DREADFULLY DEADLY HISTORY

Written by Clive Gifford
Illustrated by Andrew Pinder

Edited by Elizabeth Scoggins, Hannah Cohen
and Nicola Baxter
Designed by Barbara Ward and Zoe Bradley

DREADFULLY DEADLY HISTORY

Buster Books

First published in Great Britain in 2012 by Buster Books,
an imprint of Michael O'Mara Books Limited,
9 Lion Yard, Tremadoc Road, London SW4 7NQ

www.busterbooks.co.uk

A CIP catalogue record for this book is available from the British Library.

ISBN: 978-1-78055-032-9 in paperback print format
ISBN: 978-1-78055-127-2 in EPub format
ISBN: 978-1-78055-128-9 in Mobipocket format

1 3 5 7 9 10 8 6 4 2

Papers used by Michael O'Mara Books are natural, recyclable products
made from wood grown in sustainable forests. The manufacturing processes
conform to the environmental regulations of the country of origin.

Printed and bound in August 2012 by CPI Group (UK) Ltd,
108 Beddington Lane, Croydon, CR0 4YY, United Kingdom

CONTENTS

ENTER AT YOUR OWN RISK ...

Welcome to the most gory, gross and downright gruesome collection of facts and stories about death, doom and destruction!

From mummies and murderers, accidents and autopsies, to blood, bones and body bits, this bumper book of death has it all, but be warned, it's not for the faint hearted.

There are hundreds of facts and haunting tales to freak out your friends, plus dead cool things to make, too. If you come across a word you don't understand, check out the 'Dreadfully Deadly Definitions' on page 204.

Are you brave enough to discover history's deadliest bits? Read this book if you dare ...

EIGHT MORBID MUSEUMS

If you find yourself on a wet day with nothing weird to do, check out one of these monstrous museums.

1. The Museum Of Funeral Carriages, Barcelona, Spain.

2. The Museum Of Torture, Amsterdam, The Netherlands.

3. The National Museum Of Funeral History, Houston, Texas, USA.

4. The Museum Of Death, Hollywood, California, USA.

5. The Mummy Museum, Guanajuato, Mexico.

6. The Medieval Torture Museum, San Gimignano, Italy.

7. The London Dungeon, London, England.

8. The Vienna Undertakers' Museum, Vienna, Austria.

ANCIENT ROMAN RITES

In ancient Rome, when someone died, a number of rituals were performed before the body was taken from the home and buried or cremated.

1. A family member, often the eldest son, performed the *conclamatio* – leaning over the body and calling the dead person's name to make sure they were really dead and not just pretending.

2. The eyes of the dead person were then closed.

3. The body was washed with warm water, and the legs and arms were straightened out.

4. If the deceased held an important position in the Roman Empire, a wax impression of their face was taken so that a sculpture could be made later.

5. The body was dressed in a toga and placed on a funeral couch with flowers around it.

6. Branches from mountain pine or cypress trees were pushed into the ground outside the front door to let passers-by know that someone had died.

7. In some cases, a coin was placed with the body, usually in the mouth. This was to pay Charon, the ferryman. In Roman mythology, he was the god who transported dead Romans across the River Styx to Hades, the Underworld.

A DISAPPOINTING DEATH

In 1911, daredevil Bobby Leach sailed over the gigantic Niagara Falls in the USA in a barrel and survived.

He went on to perform many other death-defying stunts.

However, in 1926, he died after slipping on a piece of orange peel.

FEET FIRST

In 19th-century Europe and America, a dead person was usually carried out of the house feet first. This was to stop the spirit of the dead person looking back into the house and calling another member of the family to come with them.

Photographs or paintings of family members were also placed face down or covered, so that the dead person could not possess them.

Bella In The Wych-Elm

In April 1943, four boys playing in Hagley Wood in Worcestershire, England, came across a hollowed-out wych-elm tree and made a gruesome discovery. Inside was the body of a woman.

Scientists and police examined the remains but could not trace who she was. She soon gained the nickname 'Belladonna'. To this day there are rumours that she was a witch or was killed by witches, or that she stumbled across a German spy ring. No one knows, but eight months after her body was discovered, strange messages started to be found locally, scrawled in all sorts of places and asking, 'Who put Bella in the wych-elm?'.

MAKE A MUMMY IN EIGHT SIMPLE STEPS

Throughout history, people have had different ideas about what to do with the bodies of people who have died. One method that was especially popular in ancient Egypt was to mummify dead friends or relatives, to keep them fresh as a daisy for all eternity. Here's how they did it:

1. First, you have to get the body ready for 'embalming' – preserving the flesh, so it doesn't rot away. You'll need a long hook, a knife, some salt called natron, some 'canopic' jars, to store the body parts in, and a strong stomach!

2. Start by pushing the hook into the nose of the body, towards the brain. The hook should help you to break up the brain matter, so you can pull it out through the nostril.

3. Take the knife and cut a slit in the side of the body to get to the organs.

4. Pull out the lungs, liver, stomach and intestines, but leave the heart (the Egyptians

believed the dead would
need it later). Use the natron
to dry the organs and store
each one in a separate
canopic jar.

A cat amulet

5. Pack natron in and around
the body and leave it to dry
for 40 days.

6. While you are waiting, you might use your time effectively
by choosing some amulets to wrap up with the body.

7. Once the body is dry and odour-free, you need to stuff it
with linen, sawdust, herbs, spices and more natron, then sew
up the gap.

8. Now get wrapping! Cover the body completely in
bandages. You'll need to use several layers – place an amulet
between each layer.

The body is now ready to be placed in a tomb.

MIND-BOGGLING BOG PEOPLE

Some bogs (wet, marshy places) in colder parts of northern Europe are great at preserving dead human bodies. There are lots of reasons for this, from the lack of oxygen in a bog (oxygen helps the body rot away) to some bogs being acidic and helping to 'pickle' and preserve a body.

Tollund Man
This 2,400-year-old bog body is so well-preserved that you can see all of his facial features. Experts think he was killed by being hanged, as a rope was still around his neck when his body was discovered in Denmark in 1950.

Clonycavan Man
This bog body, found in Ireland in 2003, was examined by Irish police experts. It seems he was murdered, possibly by an axe, around 2,300 years ago.

Yde Girl
Another murder victim, this 2,200-year-old bog body was found in the Netherlands. She was strangled and stabbed as a teenager.

Koelbjerg Woman
Found in a Danish bog, she is the oldest known bog person. She died over 10,000 years ago but was only 20–25 when she died. Her body lay in water after death, so it wasn't mummified, but later the bog preserved her bones.

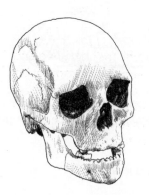

TOWER TERRORS

If you were locked up in the Tower of London, in England, in the times of the Tudors, then you had every reason to be terrified. Only a small number of important prisoners were sent there by the king or queen, but some never left the Tower alive. During King Henry VIII's reign, 69 people imprisoned in the Tower were executed.

CORPSE COMPANIONS

Ancient Egyptians were so fond of their pets that many would have their dead cats, dogs and monkeys mummified and buried in their own tombs.

In fact, lots of animals were sacred to the ancient Egyptians. Tons of them were mummified just like people and placed in tombs alongside their owners. Mummified pets that archaeologists have found include …

… a dog
… a hippo
… a hawk
… a gazelle
… an ibis (a bird)

… a crocodile
… a lizard
… a fish
… a beetle
… an antelope.

A QUEEN WITH NO HEAD

Marie-Antoinette was not an everyday queen. She arrived in France at the age of 14 and was married to the future king.

Just a few years later, her husband became King Louis XVI and Marie-Antoinette was queen. Not too happy with Louis, she distracted herself with the most frivolous and expensive activities she could find. Unfortunately, this didn't go down well with ordinary people, who hadn't been fond of the young queen in the first place.

Many people in France were extremely poor, and Marie-Antoinette became known as Madame Deficit, meaning that they blamed her for the country's debts.

In 1789, revolution broke out. People demanded an end to the monarchy and the royal family was imprisoned. After a disastrous escape attempt, Louis was put on trial and beheaded in 1793.

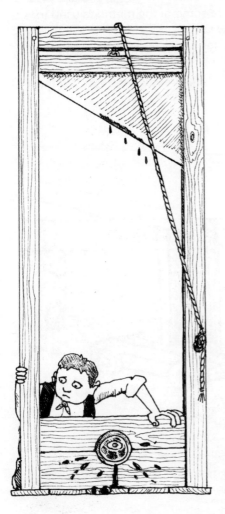

Marie-Antoinette went to the guillotine later that year, and is said to have apologized for stepping on the foot of the executioner.

LA GUILLOTINE

The guillotine was first used in France in 1792. The idea was that anyone executed should be killed in the same way, however rich or poor they were. It was last used in 1977, before the death penalty was banned in France.

WAYS TO TEST A WITCH

In medieval times, any woman who happened to live by herself and enjoy a spot of gardening might be suspected of being a witch. If she had an unpleasant wart or mole, then she was in real trouble. Here are some of the methods used to decide if someone was a witch:

Pricking The Flesh
A suspicious-looking wart or mole would be pricked with a needle. If it bled, the 'witch' was innocent.

Scales Of Justice
The accused woman would be weighed against a Bible
– if she was heavier, she was certainly evil.

Ducking
The 'witch' would be tied to a device called a ducking stool
and plunged into water. If she floated, she was guilty – if she
drowned, she was innocent (but dead!).

In any case, if the woman was found guilty, she was burned.

MAKE YOUR OWN HANDY POMANDER

In medieval times, everyone was pretty stinky even before they caught diseases. In times of plague (widespread disease), dead bodies tended to pile up, so their pong was added to the general smelliness. If you could afford an orange – in those days, you couldn't just pop to the supermarket for a bagful – a sweet-smelling 'pomander' would help keep the stench at bay. Here's how to make one:

You will need:

- 20–25g (¾oz) cloves • a tablespoon each of cinnamon, nutmeg and ground cloves • 4 drops of sandalwood oil (a natural preservative) • an orange • sticky tape • a toothpick • ribbons for hanging • a paper bag.

1. Mix the spices and oil in a bowl and put to one side.

2. Wrap tape around the orange in a criss-cross design to mark the place for the ribbon.

3. Use the toothpick to poke a hole in the orange, close to the tape. Push a clove into it.

4. Add more cloves, as close together as you can, until all the sections are covered.

5. Tip the spice mix into a paper bag, remove the tape and pop the orange into the bag. Move the orange around in the spices until it's completely covered.

6. Now leave the orange, still in the bag, in a cool, dark, dry place for several weeks. Shake the orange gently in the bag once a day.

7. Once it's dry, take the orange out of the bag and shake off any loose spice. Tie two pieces of ribbon around it, making a loop at the top.

You'll now be able to ward off any unpleasant plague-y, deathly smells, or if you prefer, use it as a Christmas decoration.

$30,000

The world's most expensive coffin in production today costs a whopping $30,000. It's made of solid bronze, covered in 14-carat gold and lined with blue velvet. Singer James Brown and pop legend Michael Jackson were both buried in a coffin like this.

IT'S TOO GOOD TO BURY.

BOX TOXIC

Beautiful, but oh-so-deadly, the box jellyfish (also called a sea wasp) has up to 60 tentacles, each covered in around 5,000 stinging cells, called nematocysts. The venom these contain is deadly. Less than three grams (1/10oz) of the stuff would be enough to kill 60 humans. Since records were first kept in the 1950s, there have been over 5,500 reported human deaths from box jellyfish stings.

ANIMALS ASSOCIATED WITH DEATH

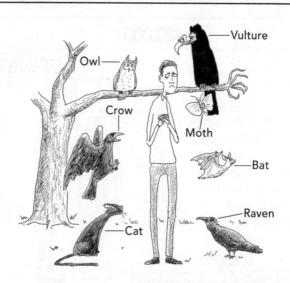

Vulture

Owl

Crow

Moth

Bat

Raven

Cat

THE AMERICAN CIVIL WAR

The American Civil War (1861–1865) is the deadliest war to have taken place in North America. It was fought between two sides, known as the Confederacy and the Union. It is now thought that around 750,000 people died during the conflict, but not necessarily because they killed each other!

As many as three out of five deaths on the Union side were said to be down to disease rather than battle injuries.

According to official records, 64 Union soldiers were executed by the Confederate forces after being captured. But the sun posed a higher risk – 313 Union soldiers died of sunstroke during the war.

QUICK, MEN, BREAK OUT THE SUNBLOCK!

THREE ENORMOUS EXPLOSIVE ERUPTIONS

Mount Tambora, Indonesia, 1815
Death toll: *more than 92,000 people*
Ten thousand were killed by the explosion itself, which blasted away over 1,000m (3,300ft) of the top of the mountain. So much ash was thrown up into the atmosphere that 1816 was the coldest year in centuries over the whole planet. Crops failed, food was short and thousands more people died.

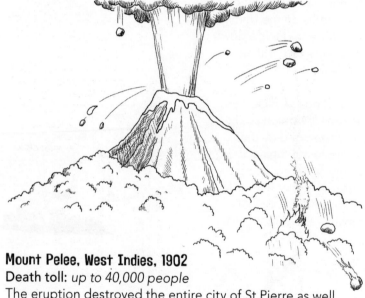

Mount Pelee, West Indies, 1902
Death toll: *up to 40,000 people*
The eruption destroyed the entire city of St Pierre as well as ships moored in the harbour and sailing nearby.

Mount Krakatoa, Indonesia, 1883
Death toll: *around 36,000 people*
More than half the island of Krakatoa was destroyed by the eruption that could be heard in Australia, over 3,000km (2,000 miles) away.

FATAL FOG

In the winter of 1952, 'smog' – a lethal mixture of fog and harmful chemicals from coal fires and traffic – descended on the streets of London, England. It was so thick that traffic had to stop, and over the next few days, at least 4,000 people died from accidents or from breathing in the poisonous fumes.

AWFUL AUTOPSIES

An autopsy, also known as a post-mortem examination, is an investigation of a corpse carried out by a 'pathologist' – a doctor skilled at figuring out how a person died.

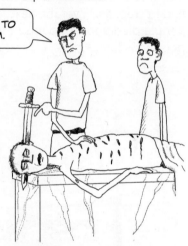

THIS ONE SEEMS TO HAVE KILLED HIM.

I Come To Examine Caesar

In 44 BC, a Roman doctor named Antistius examined the body of murdered Roman leader Julius Caesar. He reported a whopping 23 stab wounds and pinpointed the fatal one.

Off And On

King Charles I of England was beheaded in 1649 and then had his head sewn back on before being buried.

In 1813, his body underwent an autopsy by the royal surgeon, Sir Henry Halford. Once again, the unfortunate king lost part of his anatomy, as Halford kept the fourth vertebra (part of his spine) and liked to shock guests with it at dinner parties.

Getting It In The Neck

Twelve days after he assassinated US President Abraham Lincoln, John Wilkes Booth was shot in the back of the neck and killed. During his autopsy, three of his neck vertebrae had to be removed to reach the bullet.

These bones are now on display at the National Museum of Health and Medicine in Washington, DC. A rod shows the path of the bullet through the bones … if you're interested.

TOP TEN TERRIBLE TORTURES

Torture has been used throughout history to force people to say things they don't want to, or simply to punish them. The following terrible tortures tended to end in death. Unfortunate victims could be …

… covered with honey and left for insects to eat.

… stretched on a torture device called the rack until every joint was dislocated.

… tied to a large wheel and beaten to death.

… put inside an 'iron maiden' – a metal suit full of spikes and blades.

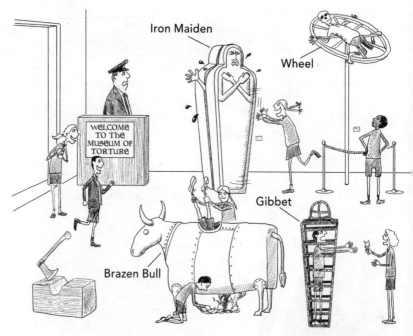

Iron Maiden

Wheel

WELCOME TO THE MUSEUM OF TORTURE

Gibbet

Brazen Bull

… cooked inside a metal container shaped like an animal – the brazen bull.

… seated with two spiked pieces of wood called the knee splitter slowly tightened around the knee (you can guess what happened).

… gibbeted (left to rot in an iron cage).

… lashed with a metal-spiked whip.

… placed in a skull crusher, which squeezed the head until the teeth broke and the brains squished out.

… tied up over bamboo shoots, which slowly and painfully grew through the body.

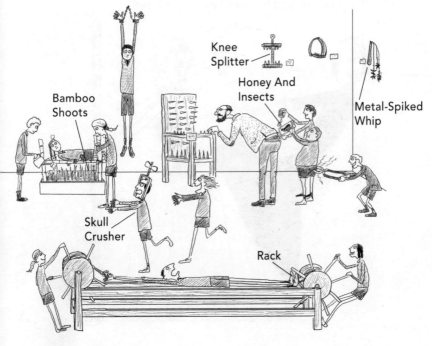

Knee Splitter

Honey And Insects

Bamboo Shoots

Metal-Spiked Whip

Skull Crusher

Rack

FASHIONS TO DIE FOR

We all know that fashion can be foolish as well as fun, but did you know that it can also be fatal?

Cruel Corsets

In the 19th and early 20th centuries, women in Europe and the United States wanted their waists to be as tiny as possible. They were laced with fearsome force into corsets strengthened with whalebone. Their inside organs were dangerously squeezed, and they could barely breathe – sometimes a life-threatening combination.

Joseph Hennella was an actor who pretended to be a woman. He became a true fashion victim when he collapsed on stage in St Louis, USA, in 1912. His over-tight corset caused breathing failure and he died two hours later.

Flaming Hoops

19th-century ladies often wore vast skirts called crinolines. Huge hoops underneath made the skirts enormous, but they were also a major fire risk. Frances Appleton, the wife of a famous American poet named Henry Wadsworth Longfellow, was burned alive when her hooped skirt caught fire in 1861.

MMM ... WHAT'S THAT LOVELY COOKING SMELL?

Doorway Disaster

In 1863, a fire in a large church in Santiago, Chile, turned into a disaster when women in hooped skirts couldn't squeeze through the exits fast enough. Their super-sized skirts blocked the doorways, resulting in the deaths of between 2,000 and 3,000 people.

FATAL FACES

Lead Then Dead

Pale couldn't fail in the past, and for several centuries high-born ladies covered their faces with white make-up called ceruse. This was an evil mixture of white lead and vinegar. The lead slowly poisoned the ladies' bodies, causing hair loss, rotting teeth and death.

Irish noblewoman Maria Gunning was just one would-be beauty who, in 1760, died of lead poisoning.

I SAY, SHE'S A STUNNER!

Beardy Weirdy

Male fashions could be just as lethal. In the 16th century, beards were all the rage. Hans Steininger was famous for having the longest beard in Austria – an incredible 1.3m (51in).

Unfortunately, when a fire broke out in 1567, Hans tried to flee but tripped over his beard, fell, broke his neck and died.

HOW TO SPOT WHEN YOU'VE GOT THE PLAGUE

Bubonic plague, or the 'Black Death', was widespread in Europe in the 14th century. People lived in terror of the disease, now thought to have been brought by fleas living on rats. Houses in cities were often so close together that the plague spread extremely easily. The chances of death were considerably more than 50:50.

Here's what you need to look out for:

☠ A fever with giddiness or light-headedness.

☠ Lymph nodes becoming lumps or 'buboes' in the neck, armpits or groin area.

☠ Blue-black splodges, caused by bleeding under the skin.

☠ The buboes developing a dotted red rash.

Risky Remedies

Plague doctors wore long beak-like masks filled with sweet-smelling herbs, which they thought would protect them from infection. The 'cures' they used included:

DON'T WORRY, DEAR. THE DOCTOR'S HERE!

HEE! HEE!

☠ Cutting open the veins so the disease can leave the body – as it bleeds to death!

☠ Cutting the buboes and putting dried human poo in them.

EUREKA ... ARRRGHH!

Some unfortunate inventors have been killed by their own inventions.

Toe Be Or Not Toe Be

William Bullock invented a rotary printing press. Unfortunately, he quite literally put his foot in it. The foot became infected with gangrene, and he died during the operation to remove it in 1867.

ER ... IT'S MEANT TO DO THIS!

Dead In Bed

In 1944, American inventor Thomas Midgley Junior accidentally strangled himself with the cord of his new invention – a pulley-operated mechanical bed.

Down And Out

In 1863, Horace Lawson Hunley, the inventor of the first combat submarine, died when his sub failed to surface.

WOW! IT GOES DOWN BEAUTIFULLY!

Failing ... And Falling

A tailor named Franz Reichelt
fell to his death from the first
deck of the Eiffel Tower, in
Paris, France, in 1912. He was
testing his new invention – an
overcoat which worked as a
parachute ... or not, as it
turned out.

Up, Up And ... Oh Dear!

Henry Smolinski had a brilliant idea – a car that could fly!
He died in 1973 when his AVE Mizar, a flying car based on a
Ford Pinto, lost its right wing strut and crashed in California.

REASONS TO AVOID TREASON

Until the 19th century, the punishment in England for a crime known as high treason (which is plotting to overthrow the country's ruler) was to be hung, drawn and quartered. There were five unpleasant stages to this method:

YOU'VE GOT TO ADMIT HE'S GOT GUTS!

1. The victim was tied to a wooden frame and dragged by horse to his execution.

2. He was hanged until nearly dead.

3. His insides were taken out and, sometimes, burned in front of him.

4. He was beheaded and cut into quarters.

5. The bits were put on show as a warning to others not to plot treason.

LOOK ON THE BRIGHT SIDE - THERE'S A GREAT VIEW!

THE DINNER OF DEATH

The last meal eaten by King Adolf Frederick of Sweden, before he died on 12ᵗʰ February 1771, was a mega-meal. No wonder he is remembered as 'The King Who Ate Himself To Death'!

Lobster

Caviar

Sauerkraut
(fermented cabbage)

Cabbage soup

Smoked herring

Champagne

14 Cream buns

Milk

Brahe's Bladder

For over 400 years, it was thought that Tycho Brahe, a brilliant Danish astronomer, died in 1601 because he was too polite to leave the table at a banquet even though he was desperate to go to the toilet!

The meal dragged on and on for hours, which gave him a serious bladder infection, and he died in great pain 11 days later.

However, scientific tests in the 1990s on some hairs from his beard showed they contained high levels of mercury, which is poisonous. Could Brahe have been poisoned by another astronomer, jealous of his success?

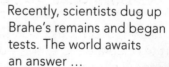

Recently, scientists dug up Brahe's remains and began tests. The world awaits an answer …

UNUSUAL URNS

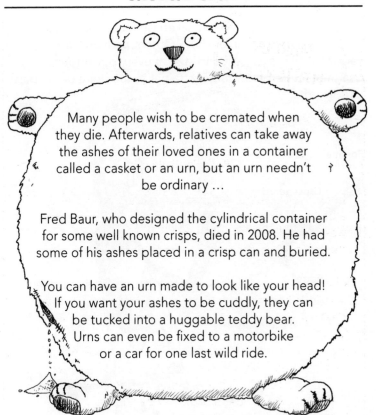

Many people wish to be cremated when they die. Afterwards, relatives can take away the ashes of their loved ones in a container called a casket or an urn, but an urn needn't be ordinary …

Fred Baur, who designed the cylindrical container for some well known crisps, died in 2008. He had some of his ashes placed in a crisp can and buried.

You can have an urn made to look like your head! If you want your ashes to be cuddly, they can be tucked into a huggable teddy bear. Urns can even be fixed to a motorbike or a car for one last wild ride.

COMPOSER TO DECOMPOSER

In 1687, a composer named Jean-Baptiste Lully conducted a concert to celebrate the recovery of King Louis XIV of France from illness. His conducting was so vigorous that he banged his staff (used before the conducting baton was invented) on his toe. The toe became infected, but Lully refused to have it cut off in an operation. The infection spread and he died.

PARTS OF A SWORD

For centuries, many men felt naked without a sword by their side. Some wore them for show. Others were only too happy to hack, slash, slit and stab at every opportunity. Use the picture below to get straight to the point of the parts of a sword!

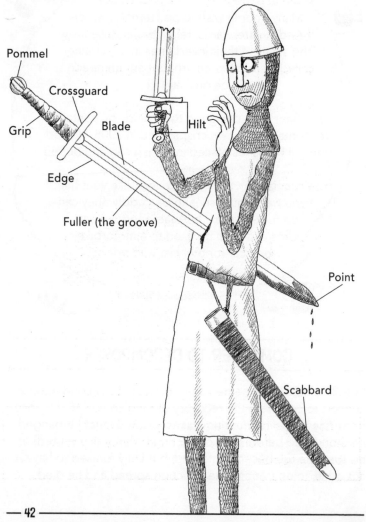

Pommel

Crossguard

Grip

Blade

Hilt

Edge

Fuller (the groove)

Point

Scabbard

TEN DEADLY POISONOUS PLANTS

Never eat:

1. Belladonna	**6.** Spurge laurel (Daphne)
2. White baneberry	**7.** Nightshade
3. Strychnine tree	**8.** Oleander
4. Castor plant	**9.** Water hemlock
5. Wolfsbane	**10.** Foxglove.

Just a single bean of the castor plant, if eaten, is enough to kill someone. It contains the highly toxic compound ricin.

LIFE DETECTOR

A Danish surgeon named Jacob Winsløw (1669–1760) was worried that ways of deciding if someone was dead were not very reliable. Here are some of the suggestions he made for tests to make absolutely sure a person was deceased:

☠ Irritating the nose with onions and garlic

☠ Whipping the skin with stinging nettles

☠ Pushing long needles under the toenails

☠ Pulling the arms and legs violently

☠ Balancing a glass of water on the chest

☠ Pouring warm wee into the mouth

☠ Tickling the nose with a feather.

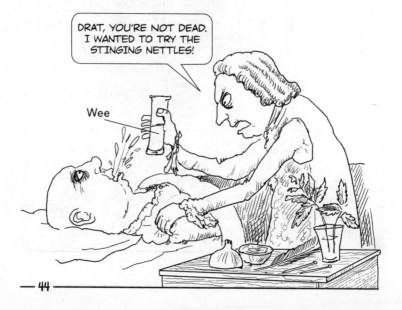

DRAT, YOU'RE NOT DEAD. I WANTED TO TRY THE STINGING NETTLES!

Wee

MIGHTY MAUSOLEUM

A mausoleum is a building that honours a person's death and usually contains their remains. The word itself comes from King Mausolus of Caria (an area that is now part of Turkey), who died in 353 BC. His wife, Artemisia, ordered a giant building to be constructed. It was known as the Mausoleum of Halicarnassus and was one of the Seven Wonders of the Ancient World. It stood for more than 1,500 years, until it was destroyed by earthquakes.

DO YOU THINK IT'S BIG ENOUGH?

American businessman John Porter Bowman built a magnificent mausoleum for his dead wife and daughters. Then he had a fine house built nearby to spend his holidays near his family. When he died in 1891, he left $50,000 to pay for his mansion to be kept just as he left it. This continued until the money ran out in the 1950s.

MUMMY POWDER

From the 12th century onwards, a powder made by grinding up ancient Egyptian mummies was sold as a medicine that could cure almost anything.

☠ French King Francis I (1494–1547) took a dose of mummy powder mixed with dried rhubarb every day. He thought it kept him strong and safe from assassins.

☠ King Charles II of England (1630–1685) often rubbed the powder on to his skin so he could absorb the ancient greatness of the pharaohs.

☠ Some artists added the powder to their paints, hoping it would give their artworks magical qualities.

☠ In the 17th and 18th centuries, demand for mummy dust was so high that crafty Egyptian merchants embalmed freshly dead people. Then they sold them as ancient mummies to foolish Europeans.

AUTOPSY TOOLKIT

Here are some of the tools doctors use to cut open a corpse and find out how and why it died.

1. Hagedorn needle – for sewing the body back up.

2. Bone saw – for slicing through larger bones.

3. Scalpel – a sharp blade to cut skin, hair and flesh.

4. Cranium chisel – to open the skull and reach the brain.

5. Rib-cutters – for cutting the ribs to reach internal organs.

6. Bread knife – for cutting out samples of the brain.

7. Scales – for weighing body parts such as the liver.

8. Enterotome – scissors for opening the intestines.

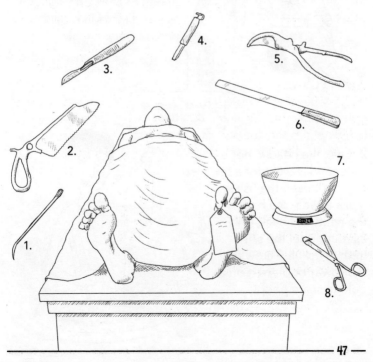

HOW TO SHRINK A HEAD

The Shuar tribe, and some other peoples living in the Amazon rainforest in South America, used to shrink the heads of enemies they had killed. Here's how they did it.
Warning: This is seriously gross. For a less bloodthirsty way of making a shrunken head, skip to pages 50 and 51.

1. First kill your enemy – use any method you like except smashing his skull.
Then cut off his head, including the neck.

3. Scrape away the flesh inside the head and sew up the eyelids. Use tiny sticks or pins to close the lips.

4. Simmer the head for a couple of hours in boiling water and herbs, until it is one third of its original size and the skin is dark and rubbery.

MMM, WHAT'S COOKING?

2. Soak the head in hot water and leave it for a few days to loosen the tissue. Make a slit in the back of the head and neck, and carefully peel the skin from the skull. Throw the skull away or place it on a pole to scare people.

5. Turn the skin inside out and scrape off any remaining flesh. Turn the skin the right way out again and sew up the slit at the back, leaving just an opening at the neck.

6. Heat some stones in a fire and drop them carefully inside the head to dry out the skin. Use hot sand in small areas such as inside the nostrils.

7. Hang the head over a fire to harden and darken it. Give the hair a trim. If you like, add coloured threads and beads to the head for decoration.

8. You will need to wear the head as a necklace or an accessory at three feasts to make sure its power passes to your tribe. After that, it makes a great decoration for your hut, or you could trade it for weapons to kill even more enemies.

Happy head shrinking!

HOW TO MAKE FRUIT FRIGHTFUL

If the instructions on pages 48 and 49 seem too gruesome, you could practise head shrinking with this recipe.

You will need:

• 1 apple (as large as possible) • a small knife
• ½ cup of table salt • 5 cups of water • 3 tablespoons of lemon juice • a piece of wire or a big paper clip (unbent)
• string • clear, matt varnish (available from hardware shops).

1. Ask an adult to help you peel the apple and carve a mouth, nose and eye sockets out of it. The facial features need to be as big as possible, as the apple will shrink.

2. Get your shrinking solution ready. In a bowl, mix the salt with the water and the lemon juice. Put the apple in the solution and let it soak for a day and a night.

3. Ask an adult to push the wire through the core of the apple, from top to bottom. Then, bend the end of the wire so that about 2.5cm (1in) of wire sits under the apple. This holds the wire in place. Bend the top of the wire to form a loop.

4. Loop some string through the wire and hang your apple head up somewhere where it can drip and dry out for several weeks … or if you're too impatient, ask an adult to help place it in a warm (not hot) oven until it is completely dry.

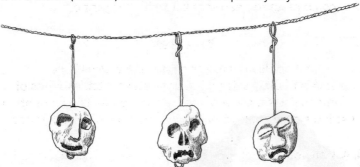

5. Finish your shrunken head by painting on features. You can glue on some fake hair, if you like. Finish it off with a coat of clear, matt varnish, then horrify friends by hanging it from your belt or up in your room.

CLUEDO® MURDER WEAPONS

Rope
Dagger
Revolver
Lead pipe
Spanner
Candlestick.

TILL DEATH DO US PART ... OR NOT!

☠ When the wife of English knight Sir John Price died in the 17th century, he had her body embalmed. Each night, he slept in his bed beside her – even when he married his second wife!

☠ Queen Juana of Spain was devastated when her husband Felipe died. She kept his body in a coffin as she travelled from Belgium to Spain and often opened it up to kiss his very dead face.

☠ Prince Pedro of Portugal had bad luck with his wives. The third one, Inez de Castro, was murdered in 1355. Pedro tracked down the men who killed her and ripped out their hearts. Legend has it that when he became king, he had her body dug up, then had her dressed in fine clothes, and crowned as his queen. Some say his courtiers were forced to kiss her dead hand.

HOW TO MAKE A FAKE CAT MUMMY

First things first – never attempt this with a real cat. It's true that the ancient Egyptians mummified almost everything, including dung-beetles, but they were particularly keen on mummifying moggies (see page 78).

Even in ancient times, though, there was dodgy dealing. No one was likely to start unwrapping feline friends, so the embalmers often just bandaged up some random bones or bits of rags. Your fake cat mummy follows a fine tradition!

You will need:

• an empty plastic bottle • a bucket of soil or sand • newspaper • masking tape • a small piece of cardboard • PVA glue • a paintbrush • cold, strong tea or coffee (no milk or sugar!) • bandages (strips of white cotton about 3cm (1in) wide from an old sheet or pillowcase are fine, or narrow gauze bandages) • paint • felt-tip pens.

1. Put some soil or sand in the bottle to make it a bit heavier. Screw up some newspaper into a ball and push it into the neck of the bottle to make a head. Tape it in place with masking tape. Do the same with a smaller ball of newspaper to make the bottom rounded.

2. Make another small ball of newspaper and tape it to the front of the head. Cut two small ears from cardboard and tape those on as well.

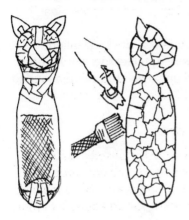

3. Mix some PVA glue half-and-half with water. Tear up bits of newspaper and glue them all over the mummy, covering up the bottle and masking tape. You will need at least two layers and more on the head to give a good cat shape. Let it dry out between layers.

4. Mix some glue with the cold, strong black tea or coffee to make a gloopy, dirty-looking mixture. Dip your bandage in it and start winding! Criss-cross the bandages on the final layer and tuck in the ends neatly.

Paint the head to match the body colour and draw on the eyes and mouth.

In the 19th century, up to 20 tons of ancient cat corpses were shipped to England for use as fertilizer.

DON'T BURY ME ALIVE!

In the past, many people were petrified of being assumed dead and buried while they were still very much alive. This fear even has a medical name: taphophobia (taf-oh-fo-be-ah). Some famous people chose weird ways to tackle their fear.

The Russian author, Fyodor Dostoevsky, was so terrified of being assumed dead when he was just sleeping that he used to leave notes beside his bed when he went to sleep, assuring people that he was not dead.

More famously strange requests:

DO NOT LET MY BODY BE PUT INTO A VAULT LESS THAN TWO DAYS AFTER I AM DEAD.

MAKE THEM CUT ME OPEN, SO I WON'T BE BURIED ALIVE.

WHEN I'M DEAD, CUT OFF MY HEAD – JUST TO BE SURE.

George Washington (US President)

Frederic Chopin (Composer)

Harriet Martineau (Writer)

GREAT EXPECTATIONS

The last wish of famous author Charles Dickens was to have a very simple and private funeral and that no one who attended should wear a scarf, cloak, black bow or 'other such revolting absurdity'. His funeral did take place with only close friends and family, but he was buried in Westminster Abbey in London, England. His grave was left open for several days so that thousands of people could pay their last respects.

TERRIBLE TYRANTS

Many rulers in the past were brutal, ruthless and delighted by death. Here is a downright deadly collection of murderous monarchs, evil emperors and rotten rulers.

IT WASN'T ME, MUM, HONEST!

Nasty Nero

The Roman emperor Nero liked to get rid of relatives. Maybe his murderous mother Agrippina had something to do with the way he turned out. She eliminated several of her son's rivals, but Nero didn't hesitate to kill her, too, when he had the chance, although it took several attempts.

Nero hired a serial killer, Locusta, to poison his brother Britannicus. He also tried to strangle his wife Octavia several times before having her veins cut so that she bled to death.

No Drinking Allowed!

The murderous Murad IV, sultan of the Ottoman Empire in the 17th century, made drinking coffee or alcohol in the city of Constantinople (in modern-day Turkey) a crime punishable by death. He sometimes performed the executions himself, using a giant weapon called a mace. He once had a group of dancing women put to death because they made too much noise.

THERE'S NOTHING LIKE A NICE CUP OF COFFEE.

NICE DAY AT THE OFFICE, DEAR?

Truly Terrible

A 16th-century ruler of Russia was known as Ivan the Terrible for a reason. He had thousands of enemies killed. Some were boiled alive, others had their arms and legs tied to four horses, which then galloped off in opposite directions. He even killed his own son by bashing him on the head with an iron-tipped staff.

WEIRD WILLS

Some people like to be in control – even when they're dead. Their last will and testament gives them one final chance to influence their nearest and dearest.

Beware Of Hair

Henry Budd had £200,000 when he died in 1862 – a large fortune at the time. All the wealth was left to his two sons – providing neither grew a moustache.

STOP YOUR SNIVELLING!

No Tears, Please!

Italian lawyer Ludovico Cortusio's will insisted that no one must weep at his cheerful funeral in 1418. If anyone did, they would find that they inherited a less-than-funny nothing at all.

Deathless Dummy

Famous ventriloquist Edgar Bergan left $10,000 to his dummy, Charlie McCarthy, to keep him in good condition. Charlie is now in the Smithsonian Institute in Washington, DC, USA.

A Quiet Life
In 1929, Californian businessman John Quincy Murray left money to two of his granddaughters – as long as they never wore jewellery or make-up, never cut their hair short, did not wear short or low-cut dresses, and never went out to the movies or dances.

Rock On!
Rock singer Janis Joplin left $2,500 in her will to pay for an all-night party in California, USA.

Holy Smoke!
Samuel Bratt's wife wouldn't allow him to smoke cigars. When he died in 1960, he bequeathed her £330,000 – as long as she smoked five cigars a day.

FAKING IT

For some people, pretending to die can be a handy way of testing their loved ones, or getting out of a sticky situation.

A Trial Run
When his tomb was completed in 1799, Timothy Dexter faked his death to see how people would react.

Some 3,000 people attended his funeral, where he revealed himself and told off his wife for not crying enough.

When Faking Backfires ...
Legend has it that in the Middle Ages, a man called John Overs faked his own death, hoping his servants would not eat for a day out of respect and save him the cost of their food. In fact, the servants cheered and raided his kitchen! Overs started telling them off, but one of the servants, thinking the devil had taken over his body, struck him with an oar and killed him.

HA HA! ONLY JOKING! ... ER ... HELLO?

DEADLY DISAPPOINTMENT

After years of planning and a tough journey across the icy mass of Antarctica, Robert Falcon Scott and his party of explorers finally reached the South Pole on 17th January 1912. The trouble was that Norwegian explorer Roald Amundsen had arrived there first, leaving behind a tent, a letter and a Norwegian flag.

Exhausted and depressed, Scott's expedition faced a hazardous 1,500km (930 mile) journey back to safety. They didn't make it. The last three members of the expedition, including Scott, died in March 1912, just 18km (11 miles) from food and supplies.

PET PALS

Some wealthy people become so close to their pets that they leave money in their wills for their pooches and pussycats to be well looked after.

A Doggy Dynasty

German countess Carlotta Liebenstein left her entire $80 million estate to her pet dog, an Alsatian called Gunther III. After Gunther III died, the estate, now worth over $200 million, passed on to another dog, Gunther IV. The pampered pooch lives with his own personal maid and chauffeur.

One Fabulous Feline

A stray cat called Tommaso became the world's richest moggie when his owner, Italian millionaire Maria Assunta, left her entire fortune of over £10 million to him in 2011.

A Hand-Fed Hound

Business tycoon Leona Hemsley left her pet dog around $12 million in her will, but her relatives went to court to overturn her wishes. The Maltese terrier, whose name was Trouble, still ended up a millionaire, being awarded $2 million. His food was brought to him on a silver tray, and each morsel was hand fed to him!

AVALANCHE!

There are an estimated one million avalanches around the world every year. Most are small and unnoticed. Some have been real killers.

☠ In 1910, trains pulling into Stevens Pass in Washington, USA, were prevented from travelling further by heavy snow. While they waited, the trains were hit by a sudden avalanche, which swept the carriages off a 40m-high (130ft) cliff, killing 96 people.

It was the worst avalanche disaster ever in the United States.

☠ On 4th September 1618, the Rodi avalanche destroyed the Swiss town of Plurs and buried 2,427 people alive. None survived.

☠ During World War I, the armies of Austria and Italy fought each other through the mountains called the Alps. In December 1916, shots fired into shifting snow triggered a series of avalanches that killed between 9,000 and 10,000 troops from both the Austrian and Italian armies.

☠ Over 2,200 years earlier in 218 BC, General Hannibal of Carthage led a giant army over the Alps on his way to attack the Romans in Italy. An avalanche wiped out around 18,000 of his men and about 2,000 of the army's horses, as well as most of its elephants.

LAST REQUESTS

☠ Magician and escapologist Harry Houdini's last request was for his wife Bess to hold a *séance* (a meeting to try to get in touch with the spirits of dead people) each year at Halloween, using ten secret words found in his will to try to contact him.

☠ The famous French general and leader Napoleon Bonaparte died in 1821. His last request asked for his head to be shaved and bits of his hair given to his friends.

I'M AFRAID MR HOUDINI IS TIED UP AT THE MOMENT.

☠ Ancient Greek poet Virgil's last request was for his epic poem *The Aeneid* to be burnt. Fortunately for lovers of poetry, his family didn't do what he asked, and the poem survived.

☠ T. M. Zink was a male American lawyer who disliked women. When he died in 1930, he left $50,000 to build a Womanless Library, which would have no books by female authors and which women would not be allowed to enter. Members of Zink's family challenged his will successfully, and the library was never built.

☠ Writer Hunter S. Thompson got his last request – for his ashes to be fired out of a cannon perched on top of a tower more than 20m (66ft) tall and shaped like a fist! The cannon was paid for by Hollywood actor Johnny Depp, who was a friend of Thompson's.

DANCING WITH THE DEAD

Every five or seven years, some of the Malagasy people of Madagascar perform a funeral tradition called *Famadihana*, which means 'the turning of the bones'.

The ceremony involves digging up the bones of dead people, which are then sprinkled with perfume or wine and danced around, while elders tell stories about the dead people to younger members of the tribe. The bones are often wrapped in new shrouds before being returned to their graves.

MOUSE MURDER

If you had bad breath in ancient Egyptian times, you might look for mice to slice. One cure for bad breath at this time was to cut a mouse in two and place one half inside your mouth.Ugh!

DEADLY DINING

Even something as simple as chowing down on some dinner has been the end for certain people.

☠ An ancient Roman senator, Lucius Fabius Cilo, is said to have died during dinner after choking on a single hair that was found in his milk.

☠ American author Sherwood Anderson died in Panama in 1941 after swallowing part of a toothpick, which punctured a hole in his digestive system.

☠ Pope Clement VII died in 1534 after eating a highly poisonous death cap mushroom. No one knows if it was an accident or something more sinister.

☠ The parents of famous scientist and thermometer-inventor Daniel Fahrenheit, both died on 14th August 1701, after eating mushrooms that turned out to be poisonous.

☠ King Henry I of England died in 1135 of food poisoning, after eating far too many stewed lampreys – eel-like creatures thought tasty at the time. He died while in France, so his remains were sewn into the skin of a bull and shipped back to England to be buried.

MMM ... I'M DYING FOR A LAMPREY!

MASS-MURDERING MAN-EATERS

Some animals, when hungry or threatened, don't hesitate to attack and kill humans. Here is a short but savage list of some of the most terrible man-chomping creatures (and they wouldn't say no to eating women and children either).

☠ In 1898, a pair of male lions attacked and killed workers building a railway line and bridge across the Tsavo River in East Africa – not just once but over and over again. In a period of nine months, 135 workers were killed by the ferocious felines. Both were finally shot and killed. One of them was 3m (10ft) long and needed eight men to carry him away.

☠ Over 60 years old, 6m (20ft) long and weighing very nearly 1,000kg (1 ton), a giant crocodile known as Gustave terrorized villagers in Burundi in Africa. He was last sighted in 2008. By then, he had attacked and killed over 300 men, women and children.

☠ A male leopard living in the Kumaon region of India killed over 400 people before it was shot in 1910. It was nicknamed the 'Panar Leopard'. It seems the leopard was injured and found it hard to catch and kill wild animals. Instead, it hunted humans.

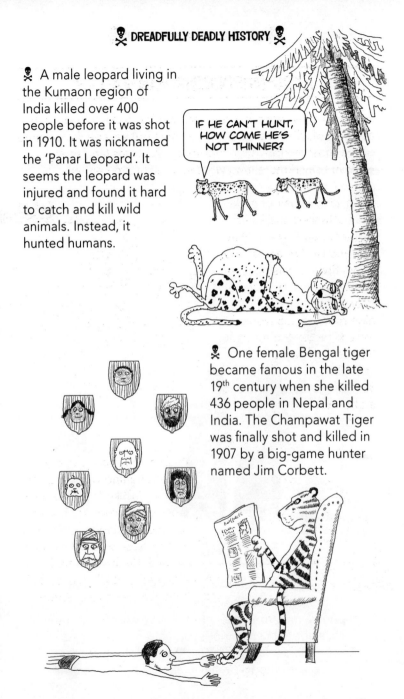

IF HE CAN'T HUNT, HOW COME HE'S NOT THINNER?

☠ One female Bengal tiger became famous in the late 19th century when she killed 436 people in Nepal and India. The Champawat Tiger was finally shot and killed in 1907 by a big-game hunter named Jim Corbett.

PRETTY NAUGHTY POLLY

In 1845, at the funeral of Andrew Jackson, the seventh president of the United States, it is said that his pet parrot, Pol, attended. The bird had to be removed from the ceremony when he started swearing in English and Spanish. Could he have learnt these rude words from the president?

FEARSOME PHOBIAS

Coimetrophobia (coy-met-ro-fo-be-ah) – fear of cemeteries
Myctophobia (mic-to-fo-be-ah) – fear of darkness
Necrophobia (nec-ro-fo-be-ah) – fear of death or dead things
Phasmophobia (fas-mo-fo-be-ah) – fear of ghosts
Placophobia (plak-oh-fo-be-ah) – fear of tombstones
Tomophobia (to-mo-fo-be-ah) – fear of surgical operations.

DEATH OF A PRESIDENT

Eight US presidents have died in office. Seven of them were elected in a year ending in zero, and the other one died in a year ending in zero. Weird!

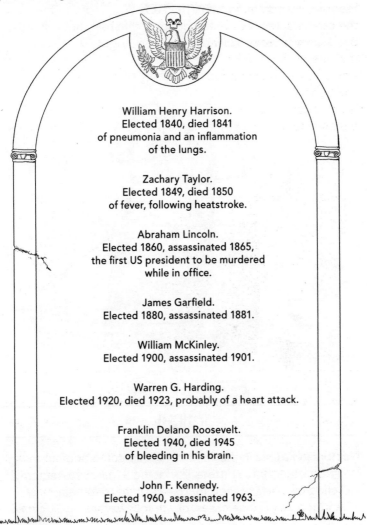

William Henry Harrison.
Elected 1840, died 1841
of pneumonia and an inflammation
of the lungs.

Zachary Taylor.
Elected 1849, died 1850
of fever, following heatstroke.

Abraham Lincoln.
Elected 1860, assassinated 1865,
the first US president to be murdered
while in office.

James Garfield.
Elected 1880, assassinated 1881.

William McKinley.
Elected 1900, assassinated 1901.

Warren G. Harding.
Elected 1920, died 1923, probably of a heart attack.

Franklin Delano Roosevelt.
Elected 1940, died 1945
of bleeding in his brain.

John F. Kennedy.
Elected 1960, assassinated 1963.

OOPS!

Is this the worst luck ever? In 1794, the crew of the *Jackal* fired a 13-gun salute in honour of John Kendrick, a famous American sea captain and explorer. John Kendrick was moored close by in his boat, the *Lady Washington*. One of the cannons was accidentally loaded with real shot instead of blanks, which hit and killed Kendrick outright.

OUCH!

Doctors in Prussia in the 18th and 19th centuries sometimes treated people who stuttered by doing a 'hemiglossectomy' – cutting off parts of their tongue! Excruciating pain, infection and, in some cases, death followed.

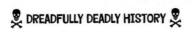

THE ROAD OF DEATH

The North Yungas Road in Bolivia is also known as *El Camino de la Muerte*, which means 'The Road of Death'.

Built by prisoners in the 1930s, the road is about 60km (37 miles) long but often only 3m (10ft) wide. It snakes around steep hills and cliffs with drops of over 500m (1,640ft) on one side and no guard rails. The danger is heightened by frequent fog and heavy rain.

As a result, around 300 people die on this horrific highway every year. Yikes!

PET MATTERS

It wasn't only the ancient Egyptians who were fond of their pets (see page 54 for some mummified moggies). Animal lovers throughout history have grieved when their pets passed away.

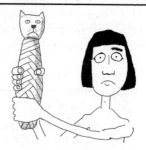

☠ Alexander the Great (356–323 BC) owned a dog called Peritas. It is said that when she died, he led a large funeral procession to her grave, erected a stone monument, and ordered those who lived nearby to celebrate her memory every year.

☠ Cyrus the Great (580–529 BC) was a king of ancient Persia. He got so upset when one of his favourite horses drowned that he sentenced the offending river to 'death'. A tricky execution to carry out? Not at all. Cyrus had channels dug so that the river drained to a shallow depth in which no horse could drown.

I DON'T THINK THIS IS WORKING, SIRE.

☠ When Pope Leo X's favourite pet, Hanno, died in 1516 he was buried in the Belvedere courtyard in the Vatican in Rome, Italy. The Pope wrote a poem about his lost pet and also commissioned the famous painter Raphael to paint a series of scenes commemorating Hanno's life. Hanno was an elephant!

☠ The *Cimetière des Chiens*, a pet cemetery, opened in Paris, France, in 1899. More than 40,000 pets are buried there. The most famous is Rin Tin Tin, a dog who starred in 26 Hollywood films before his death in 1932. The *Cimetière des Chiens* may not be the oldest pet cemetery though. Recent archaeological digs at Ashkelon in Israel revealed a dog cemetery that dates back over 2,000 years.

EXPIRING EXPLORERS

Exploration has always been a risky business. When brave (sometimes foolhardy) adventurers set off into the unknown, some of them are almost certain not to come back.

Captain James Cook
This famous British sea captain had mapped much of Australia's eastern coast and parts of the Pacific Ocean, and lived to tell the tale. In 1779 he went back to Kealakekua Bay in the Hawaiian Islands for ship repairs, where fights broke out and he was killed. As a mark of respect, local chiefs cooked his body so that his bones could be cleaned and kept.

David Livingstone
In 1883, Livingstone, a Scottish explorer of parts of central Africa, died in the village of Illala in modern day Zambia from malaria and internal bleeding caused by truly dreadful diarrhoea. Yuck!

Juan De La Cosa

This Spanish sailor made some of the first ever maps of the coastline of the Americas. He was killed in Cartagena, Colombia, in 1509, by poison darts and arrows fired by hostile locals.

OW! BLOOMIN' MOSQUITOS!

Burke And Wills

Robert Burke and William Wills headed an ill-fated expedition to cross Australia from south to north. The explorers took with them over 90kg (200lbs) of soap, 1,300kg (1.4 tons) of sugar, 180kg (400lbs) of bacon and a Chinese dinner gong. Somehow, the pair managed to die of starvation on the way back from northern Australia in 1861.

I WISH WE HADN'T EATEN IT ALL IN THE FIRST WEEK.

WE'VE STILL GOT THE SOAP.

Robert De La Salle

La Salle was a French explorer who travelled around the Great Lakes of North America and parts of the southern United States. In 1687, while he was exploring Texas, some members of his expedition turned against him and shot him dead.

HOT STUFF

According to legend, ancient Roman general Marcus Licinius Crassus was killed in around 53 BC by the Parthians from ancient Persia, who poured molten gold down his corpse's throat – as a symbol of the general's greed.

CREATIVE COFFINS

The Ga-Adangbe people from the West African nation of Ghana are famous for their fancy funerals. They make coffins that match the dead person's interests or requests. Coffins have been made in the shape of ...

... a mobile phone
... a taxi cab
... a large fish
... a lion
... a crab
... a pineapple
... an airliner
... a fizzy drink bottle
... a peacock
... a trainer.

FAMOUS LAST WORDS

'Go away. I'm all right.'
(H.G. Wells, science-fiction author, 1946)

'Don't let it end like this! Tell them I said something!'
(Pancho Villa, Mexican revolutionary, to a nearby journalist as
he died from a bullet wound, 1923)

'Am I dying or is this my birthday?'
(Lady Astor, seeing her bed surrounded by relatives, 1964)

'They couldn't hit an elephant at this dist ...'
(General John Sedgwick, misjudging the aim of Confederate
soldiers he was fighting in the American Civil War, 1864)

HOW TO MAKE A BRASS RUBBING

Many tombs or monuments to dead people have words and pictures engraved on them, either on brass plates or on the stone itself. You can make a copy of these by laying a piece of paper on them and rubbing over them gently with a crayon.

You will need:

• a soft brush or cloth • strong but thin paper
• wax crayons • masking tape
• permission from the clergyman or caretaker.

1. Use the soft brush or cloth to clear the surface of dust or grit that might tear the paper.

3. Using the long side of the crayon, rub very gently over the object in one direction until all the engraving shows on the paper.

2. Place the paper over the words or pictures and use masking tape to make sure it can't move.

4. Remove the masking tape slowly and carefully and lift the paper away.

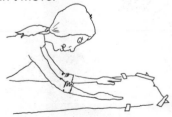

☠ Experiment with colours. Gold or white crayon on black paper is good.

FIT FOR A (DEAD) QUEEN

Emperor Shah Jahan ordered an amazing tomb in memory of his wife Mumtaz Mahal, who died giving birth to the couple's fourteenth child in 1631. It took 22 years and 20,000 workers to complete it, and the Taj Mahal, in Agra, India, is one of the world's most famous and beautiful buildings. It is, however, not certain that Mumtaz is actually buried there.

SCARED OF THE DARK

Emperor Louis the Pious was the son of a man named Charlemagne, who was King of the Franks. In 840, the sky became totally dark in the daytime, during a solar eclipse. Five minutes later, daylight returned, but according to legend, Louis didn't. He had died of fright.

VIOLENT VESUVIUS

On a summer morning in AD 79, people who lived in and near the town of Pompeii on the Italian coast woke up as usual. Within hours, their world split apart when the mountain that stood behind the town blasted into horrific life.

Local people didn't know Vesuvius was a volcano. It hadn't erupted for 1,800 years. They didn't even have a word in Latin for 'volcano'.

Before the massive eruption, there had been several signs of approaching disaster, such as small earthquakes. No one was killed by red hot lava gushing down the slopes of Vesuvius. There wasn't any. Instead, super-heated gas, 'magma' (molten rock) and ash rose high into the air, where it cooled – then fell as ash and rock.

Pompeii was buried in the hot ash, killing many people instantly.

Archaeologists have worked to uncover this buried town, which was preserved by the ash that covered it. The skeletal remains of people and even animals have been discovered, frozen where they fell, thousands of years ago.

MAKE YOUR OWN VOLCANO

You will need:

- a tray • modelling clay, papier-mâché or soil
- a plastic bottle or container
- 1–2 tablespoons bicarbonate of soda (baking soda)
- red food dye • 30ml (⅛ cup) vinegar
- washing-up liquid.

1. Build a cone-shaped volcano on the tray. You can make this from modelling clay, papier-mâché or soil from the garden. Leave an opening in the middle, big enough for your plastic container to fit inside.

2. Put the bicarbonate of soda (baking soda) and a few drops of food dye into your plastic container. Add three or four drops of washing-up liquid. Top up the bottle with warm water, but leave space for the vinegar.

3. Put the bottle in the middle of your volcano and quickly pour in the vinegar in one go. Stand back and watch the volcano erupt. The vinegar and bicarbonate of soda react with one another to make carbon dioxide gas. Red 'lava' should bubble up and run down the sides of your erupting volcano.

UNSPORTING ENDS

There's nothing wrong with a bit of healthy competition, but sometimes sports can get a bit more sinister …

A Hollow Victory

At the ancient Greek Olympics in 564 BC, Arrichion of Phigaleia's throat was crushed by his opponent in the *pankration* (a brutal form of wrestling) just as his opponent submitted and lost the bout. Arrichion was proclaimed the winner, even though he was dead.

The Game Of Their Lives

The ancient Aztecs played a ball game called *ullamalitzli*. Two teams would try to get a ball through stone rings. The captain of the losing team, and sometimes all his team-mates, could be killed as sacrifices at the end of the game.

IT WAS OFFSIDE, I TELL YOU …

This book should be returned/renewed by the latest date shown above. Overdue items incur charges which prevent self-service renewals. Please contact the library.

Wandsworth Libraries
24 hour Renewal Hotline
01527 852385
www.wandsworth.gov.uk

Wandsworth

The Dangerous Game
In 1896, Arsenal Football Club's first ever captain, Joseph Powell, fell awkwardly and broke his arm during a match against Kettering Town. The arm was amputated, but he died of an infection within a week of the match.

IT'S JUST AN 'ARMLESS SCRATCH!

Better A Sweater!
Marathon runner Francisco Lázaro of Portugal was competing at the 1912 Olympics in Stockholm, Sweden, when he collapsed and became the first modern Olympian to die during an event. The wax he had used all over his body to stop himself sweating caused the minerals in his body, called electrolytes, to become imbalanced, which caused his death.

IT'S VERY SAD, BUT HE POLISHES UP BEAUTIFULLY.

COFFIN CAPERS

A Kitchen Coffin

James 'Jemmy' Hirst was an 18th century English farmer who kept a coffin propped up in his kitchen. He would invite people to stand in the coffin, lock them in, and then charge them a penny to be let out.

A Temporary Coffin

In Thailand, some Buddhist temples perform a ritual where a living person dresses in black and lies in a coffin for a few minutes, while monks perform chants and prayers to rid them of bad luck and to help prolong their life.

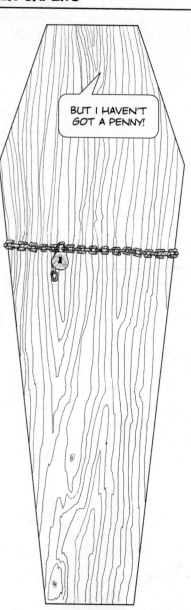

BUT I HAVEN'T GOT A PENNY!

BACK FROM THE DEAD?

Roger Tichborne was a very rich young man from a noble family in England. In 1854 he set sail for the West Indies, but there was a shipwreck, and poor Roger was presumed dead.

Years passed, then suddenly, in 1866, Roger's mother received a letter from Australia, from a man claiming to be her son. She was delighted, and immediately invited him to come home to the family. But before he could take his place as heir to the Tichborne fortune, he had to prove who he was in court.

The man became known as 'the Tichborne claimant', and after a long and dramatic court case, it was decided that he was a liar, and he was sent to prison. However, he certainly seemed to know a lot of secrets about the Tichborne family, and even to this day his true identity has remained somewhat of a mystery. Could Roger have come back from the dead after all?

DANGER SIGNS

Deadly chemicals are transported all over the world by air, road, rail and sea. In case of an accident, it's important that the emergency services know what they're dealing with. International symbols have been developed so that anyone, anywhere can be forewarned.

Danger: may
catch fire

Danger: highly
poisonous

Danger: may harm
the environment

Danger: may
seriously harm health

Danger: gas under
pressure

Danger: explosive
material

Danger: may cause
health difficulties

Danger: may cause or
worsen fire

Danger: corrosive (may
burn what it touches)

IT'S NUTS!

More people are killed each year by coconuts falling on their heads than by sharks.

THE MAN WITH TWO HEADS

Famous classical composer Joseph Haydn died in 1809 and was buried in Hundsturm Cemetery on the outskirts of Vienna, Austria. Shortly after his funeral, two men, Joseph Rosenbaum and Johann Peter, broke into Haydn's grave and cut off his head. They were enthusiastic 'phrenologists' – people who think that studying the bumps on someone's head can give clues to their personality.

The daring duo hid the head under a straw mattress but found themselves under suspicion. When questioned, Rosenbaum gave the authorities a different head, which was then buried with Haydn's headless body.

Haydn's real head wasn't reunited with his body until 1954. Both heads were put on display in Eisenstadt in Austria in 2009 to mark the 200th anniversary of his death.

COLOURS OF MOURNING

In many Western countries, people traditionally wear black clothes after someone close to them has died, to show that they are in mourning for their loved one. But in some cultures, it's all about the colour!

☠ In South Africa, people wear red clothes to funerals, as this colour is associated with sadness and loss.

☠ Rather than wearing white to a wedding, Japanese mourners dress in white clothes when someone has died. Often they wear a white carnation, too.

☠ Purple is the traditional colour of mourning in Thailand – but not for everybody. Widows mourning their husbands can be seen wearing purple.

☠ Although it might seem bright and sunny, in Egypt and Myanmar it's yellow that is associated with death and mourning, and is the suitable colour to wear to a funeral.

EINSTEIN'S BRILLIANT BRAIN

When it comes to clever people, few are thought of as brainier than the brilliant scientist Albert Einstein. When he died in 1955, his brain was removed by Thomas Harvey who weighed it as 1.23kg (2.7lbs).

Some of the brain was cut into thin slices to be examined on microscope slides, but Harvey kept the rest of the brain in a jar at home. The brain survived many house moves around the United States before finally being given to the University of Princeton.

BODY SNATCHERS!

Medical students and researchers learn a lot by 'dissecting' – cutting up – dead bodies. In the past, medical schools paid good money for bodies and sometimes didn't ask too many questions.

☠ Four medical students in the Italian city of Bologna were caught digging up the recently buried body of a criminal as long ago as 1319.

☠ In the 19th century, about 200 body snatchers were at work in London. In 1830–31 alone, seven bodysnatching gangs were caught by police.

☠ In the 18th and 19th centuries, hundreds of bodies were snatched from the Bully's Acre Cemetery in Dublin for Irish medical schools – perhaps as many as 2,000.

NO, OFFICER, I'M JUST TAKING MY DEAR OLD MOTHER FOR A WALK.

☠ William Burke and William Hare were notorious body snatchers in Edinburgh in the early 19th century, selling corpses to doctors and surgeons. When they struggled to find newly buried bodies, they started murdering people. Burke was found guilty of murder and hanged in 1829. Then his body was given to medical science for a taste of his own medicine.

HEART TO HEART

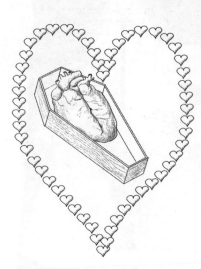

Together Forever

Famous writer Thomas Hardy wanted to be buried with his first wife, Emma, in Stinsford, England. After his death, in 1928, a friend insisted that Westminster Abbey in London was a more fitting place for his burial. A compromise was found that kept everyone happy. Hardy's body was cremated, and the ashes were buried in Westminster Abbey, but his heart was buried with Emma, as he had wished.

A Tasty Morsel

During the French Revolution, the tomb of the French King Louis XIV was broken into, and his heart was stolen. It was later eaten by the eccentric English scientist William Buckland, who made a habit of eating unusual foods.

Poetic Hearts

The poet Lord Byron died in Mesolongi in Greece in 1824. His heart was cut out and buried there, but the rest of his body was sent to England.

OH, JUST WHAT I'VE ALWAYS WANTED!

Two years earlier, Byron had been present at the cremation of another writer, Percy Bysshe Shelley, in Italy. Shelley's heart was snatched from the cremation fire and given to his wife, Mary Shelley – the author of *Frankenstein*. When their son (also Percy) died in 1889, his father's heart was found among his belongings and buried in Bournemouth.

AN EMPEROR'S END

Emperor Andronikos I Komnenos ruled the Byzantine Empire in the 12th century. His death by an angry mob in Constantinople (now Istanbul, Turkey) was particularly gruesome. Over three days, the mob ran through a menu of terrible tortures …

☠ He was beaten.

☠ His teeth were pulled out.

☠ His eyes were gouged out.

☠ He was hung up by his feet and slowly hacked to pieces until he died.

Not a great end for an emperor … or anyone else really!

THE DAY OF THE DEAD

All Saints' Day falls on 1st November each year. In Mexico, this is known as *Dia de los Muertos* in Spanish – 'Day of the Dead'. It is a day when dead friends and family members are remembered.

Far from being sad or scary, this day is a celebration. People wear wooden skull masks called *calacas*, bring gifts to the dead people's graves and dance in honour of their relatives.

Special food is made and eaten, such as sugary sweets in the shape of skulls and *pan de muerto* – 'bread of the dead' – which may be decorated with small dough teardrops or bone shapes (see pages 160–161 to find out how to make your own). An altar is often made in the home and decorated with candles and photos of the dead loved ones.

AN ARMY FOR A (DEAD) EMPEROR

In 1974, farmers in Xi'an, China, found the giant underground tomb of the first Emperor of China, Qin Shi Huangdi. The tomb is still being excavated, but it is full of amazing life-size statues, all made of terracotta – a kind of clay. It is said that they were made to guard and protect the Emperor after death.

Qin Shi Huangdi spent much of his life trying to find an 'elixir of life' – a medicine that would mean he would never die. He never found it, but took mercury to try to live longer. Mercury is poisonous so this is, in fact, probably what killed him.

There are probably 8,000 terracotta warriors in the tomb. Only a fraction have been excavated so far. There are also hundreds of statues of horses, chariots and even acrobats.

In the earth, the statues are brightly coloured. They turn grey when exposed to the air.

THE EMPEROR'S GONE OFF WARRIOR STATUES. BURY 'EM!

BODY PARTS AND PARTED BODIES

☠ For almost 30 years after the beheading of Sir Walter Raleigh in 1618, his wife, Elizabeth, kept his preserved head in a red leather bag.

> I'M SURE MY PURSE IS IN HERE SOMEWHERE ... OOPS!

☠ The Wilder Brain Collection is a group of more than 70 whole brains of dead people, preserved and stored at Cornell University, USA.

☠ In 2010, the Museum of the History of Science in Florence, Italy, displayed a tooth, a finger and a thumb belonging to the great scientist and telescope pioneer Galileo. They were only discovered in 2009, when an art dealer, Alberto Bruschi, bought an old wooden case and found them inside.

☠ The bladder of Italian biologist Lazzaro Spallanzani, who died in 1799, is still on display in a room of medical exhibits at the University of Pavia in Italy.

WHAT DO YOU MEAN YOU'VE LOST IT?

☠ Badu Bonsu II of the Ahanta tribe (in present day Ghana), was beheaded by Dutch soldiers in 1838. His head disappeared and was thought lost until over 150 years later, when it was found pickled in a jar in a Dutch museum. In 2009, members of the Ahanta tribe flew from Africa to the Netherlands to take the head back to Ghana.

THE WORLD'S MOST MURDEROUS CREATURE

Is it a human? Is it a lion? Is it a shark? Nope! The mosquito takes the title of the most murderous creature. Mosquitoes carry the deadly disease malaria, which infects as many as 500 million people a year. Between 500,000 and 1,000,000 people die from the disease each year.

LETHAL LEISURE

No matter how innocent a pastime or hobby may seem, things can sometimes go wrong in the deadliest of ways.

An Audience Accident
Ancient Roman gladiators often fought to the death, but those watching them were sometimes in danger as well. In AD 27, an ancient Roman amphitheatre collapsed in Fidenae, Italy. As many as 20,000 of the 50,000 audience members died.

The Show Must Go On
In 1958, a TV drama series was being filmed and transmitted live when one of the actors, Gareth Jones, died between scenes. Off camera, the director furiously scribbled on scripts, giving the actor's remaining lines to other cast members so that the show could continue to be broadcast.

A Theatrical Murder
Abraham Lincoln was the first US president to be assassinated. He was shot in 1865, while watching a play at a theatre in Washington, DC, USA.

Bullet Backfire
Chung Ling Soo was known as 'the marvellous Chinese conjuror'. He wasn't Chinese at all, but an American performer who pretended he didn't understand English. When he was on stage in 1918, his bullet-catching trick went disastrously wrong, and he died from a bullet wound the next day.

105

THE RAILWAY OF THE DEAD

In 1854, horse-drawn vehicles filled the streets of London, England. The London Necropolis Company built a special railway station close to Waterloo Station. Its trains carried dead bodies and mourners to the world's largest cemetery at the time – in Brookwood, Surrey, 25 miles (40km) from the centre of London.

There were ticket machines inside the station so that mourners could buy return trips on the train. The special coffin tickets for the dead body were, of course, only one way!

BLOOD-DRINKERS

Vampires with fangs and capes may well live only in books and movies, but some stories of people drinking blood are terrifyingly true.

YUM!

☠ The ancient Scythians lived in an area that now includes southern Russia and the Ukraine. It is said they drank the blood of the first enemy they killed in battle.

SORRY LADS. DOCTOR'S ORDERS.

☠ An ancient Roman scholar, Celsus, wrote a book about medicine called *De Medicina*. He claimed that epilepsy could be cured if the patient drank the blood of a dead gladiator.

☠ In 1492, Pope Innocent VIII was very ill. His doctors advised him to drink the blood of three young boys. Both he and the three boys died shortly afterwards.

☠ Some ancient Romans also believed that sipping the blood of fallen gladiators would give them strength.

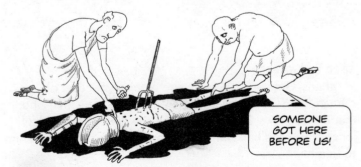

SOMEONE GOT HERE BEFORE US!

DEATH PENALTIES

Lethal Law

The first record of criminals being sentenced to death was found in the Code of King Hammurabi of Babylon, written over 3,750 years ago. Crimes punishable by death included burglary and falsely accusing someone of a crime.

Killed By Kindness

In Athens, Greece 2,700 years ago, a super-strict set of laws demanded death for many different crimes. The man who made these laws, Draco, is said to have died when grateful locals showered him with clothes and cloaks, suffocating him to death!

Beware, Bunny Burglars!
In Britain, by the 1700s, there were a staggering 222 different crimes that carried the death sentence. These included cutting down a tree, printing fake tax stamps and robbing a rabbit warren!

SERVES HIM RIGHT!

HE HASN'T LEARNT A THING!

Parsley Punishment
In 1612, the governor of British settlers in the Virginia Colony in North America brought in strict new laws, including the death penalty for crimes such as stealing herbs or grapes, trading with Native Americans, and making 'unseemly or unfitting speeches'.

WEIRD WORLD WAR I WEAPONS

The gigantic Paris Gun was a massive World War I weapon. It was more than 40m (131ft) long, and the shells it fired each weighed a whopping 120kg (265lbs). The gun was so powerful that it was placed over 100km (62 miles) from Paris, yet its shells reached the city, causing more than 250 deaths.

PARIS IS OVER THERE. YOU'VE JUST HIT BERLIN!

EVEN WEIRDER WORLD WAR II WEAPONS

☠ During World War II, the Soviet army tried to train dogs to carry anti-tank mines under German tanks. The plan was that the mine would blow up the enemy tank – and unfortunately the dog along with it. But things didn't exactly go to plan. When unleashed on the battlefield, many of the dogs simply ran away or headed for the nearest Soviet tanks!

... AND THEN YOU CRAWL UNDER THE GERMAN TANKS AND BLOW THEM UP.

YEAH, IN YOUR DREAMS!

☠ The *Yokosuka MXY-7 Okha* was a small, rocket-powered Japanese aircraft, designed as a flying bomb. Pilots would aim the plane at US warships. One such suicide mission helped to sink the warship USS *Mannert L. Abele*.

IS IT SUPPOSED TO BE COMING THIS WAY?

ARE YOU SURE THIS IS RIGHT?

☠ The *Krummlauf*, meaning 'curved barrel', was a bent gun barrel fitted to a German *Sturmgewehr 44* assault rifle – so that soldiers could shoot round corners!

☠ One truly barmy American World War II plan was to drop lots of Mexican bats, each equipped with an 'incendiary' – fire-causing – bomb, over the largely wooden cities of Japan. Timers would cause the bombs to explode after the bats had landed. Tests were carried out by the US Air Force and Navy, but the batty plan never saw action.

I THINK WE SHOULD TRY A SMALLER BOMB.

THE WHEELS ON THE HEARSE
GO ROUND AND ROUND

A hearse is a specially adapted vehicle that carries a body to its burial or cremation. One unusual vehicle used as a hearse is a 1965 London Routemaster double-decker bus. It has room for the coffin downstairs and 40 mourners upstairs.

Strangely, the man who began London buses (or 'omnibuses' as they were then called), George Shillibeer, became an undertaker when rival companies drove him out of the bus business. It is said that he, too, converted his horse-drawn buses into hearses.

DING-DONG, I'M NOT DEAD!

In the 19th century, many people were really afraid of being buried alive. Various ingenious ideas were designed to make sure people were well and truly dead when buried.

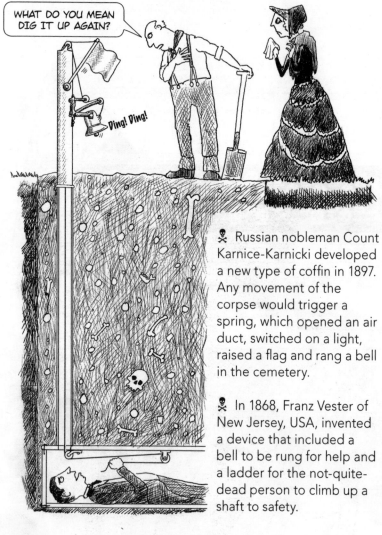

WHAT DO YOU MEAN DIG IT UP AGAIN?

Ding! Ding!

☠ Russian nobleman Count Karnice-Karnicki developed a new type of coffin in 1897. Any movement of the corpse would trigger a spring, which opened an air duct, switched on a light, raised a flag and rang a bell in the cemetery.

☠ In 1868, Franz Vester of New Jersey, USA, invented a device that included a bell to be rung for help and a ladder for the not-quite-dead person to climb up a shaft to safety.

☠ In the UK, William Tebb and others formed The Society for the Prevention of People Being Buried Alive. It encouraged people to bury crowbars, shovels and bells in their graves, so that if they happened to be alive, they could get out.

☠ In some parts of Germany in the 19th century, a simpler method was used. Dead people were laid out in a *Leichenhaus* – a 'corpse house' or mortuary – and attached to a bell by wire. If a corpse moved, the bell rang. The grim job of the staff there was to wait a few days for any sign of life, then bury the definitely-dead corpse. For a small fee in some mortuaries, members of the public could view the grisly scene.

GET YOUR TICKETS FOR THE LEICHENHAUS!

LOOKS LIKE IT'S A GOOD SHOW TODAY!

EXCRUCIATING EXECUTIONS

If you're going to be executed and there's no escape, you need a skilled executioner. A bungling beheader or a hopeless hangman doesn't bear thinking about ...

☠ Beheading by sword or axe was a quick method of execution ... unless the axe wasn't sharp or the axeman an amateur. In 1541, it took an estimated 11 blows with the axe to kill Margaret Pole, the Countess of Salisbury.

☠ William Townley was sentenced to hang for burglary in Gloucester, England, in 1811, but later the authorities sent a letter to cancel the execution. Unfortunately, it was sent to Hereford instead of Gloucester. There were no phones or cars in those days, so a horseman was sent galloping to Gloucester. He arrived 20 minutes too late – Townley's hanging was finished ... and so was he.

☠ In 1650, Anne Greene was found guilty of murdering her child and sentenced to death. She was hanged for 30 minutes in Oxford, England, and seemed to be dead. Her friends, who didn't want her to wake up later under the knife or the ground, beat her hard to make sure. She was put in a coffin and taken to a doctor to be cut open and examined, but he found she was still breathing! She recovered in a few days and was pardoned.

FATAL FIREWORKS

We all know that fireworks can be dangerous, but one organized firework display in May 1770 was truly deadly. A firework landed in the crowd that had gathered in Paris to celebrate the marriage of French King Louis XVI to Marie-Antoinette. The crowd stampeded in terror, and 133 people were killed in the crush.

THREE DEADLY DISEASES

Spanish Flu
Ordinary flu epidemics are bad enough, but this one was a 'pandemic', which means it swept the globe. Over 25 million lives worldwide were claimed by the disease.

Malaria
This might be the deadliest disease in history – it still kills at least one million people every year. Mosquitoes can carry a parasite that attacks your red blood cells. The parasite slowly kills you unless it's treated.

Smallpox
This disease causes horrible spots all over the skin and leaves nasty scars – but only if you are lucky enough to survive. Smallpox has now been wiped out, but it killed huge numbers, including 95% of some Native American populations, when the disease was brought to them by European explorers.

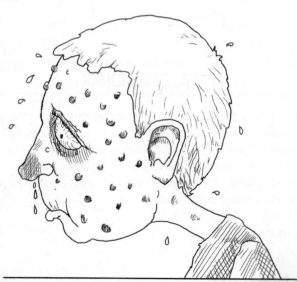

READ ALL ABOUT IT!

It's going to happen to all of us, so maybe we should read up about death beforehand. The first books about death were written a surprisingly long time ago. Here are three famous ones.

The Book Of The Dead

First produced by scribes on papyrus scrolls around 3,500 years ago, this ancient Egyptian guide to death contains many illustrations and magic spells.

The Tibetan Book Of The Dead

Created over 1,200 years ago, this collection of writings offers advice to Buddhists about how to live their lives and approach their deaths.

Ars Moriendi

First printed in the 15th century, this title translates as 'The Art Of Dying'. It was one of the first printed books in Europe and gave Christians advice about how to live and how to pray in order to die a good death.

ANIMAL ASSAULTS

Stranger Than Fiction
Aeschylus, an ancient Greek playwright, is said to have died in 456 or 455 BC when an eagle flying high above dropped a tortoise on his head. It was extraordinarily bad luck for Aeschylus – and the tortoise.

HAH! THEY WILL SUSPECT NOTHING!

OH NO!

OH NO!

OH NO!

Violent Vermin
During World War II, members of the resistance network fighting Germany and its allies in Europe filled dead rats with explosives. The plan was to put the dead rats on piles of coal at railway stations, so that when they were loaded into the boiler of a steam train, they would explode. However, the plan was foiled by the Germans the first time it was used.

Monkey Business

King Alexander I of Greece died in 1920 after being bitten by a monkey in the Royal Gardens in Athens, where he had been walking his dog. He died of an infection four weeks later.

I SAID THEY'D NEED STRONGER CHAINS.

Jumbo Justice

A circus elephant called Mary killed her new handler, Walter 'Red' Eldridge, in 1916. She was executed for her crime – hanged from a large railway crane in Erwin, Tennessee, USA – the very next day.

TAKE IT TO THE GRAVE

Some people have insisted on being buried with possessions that meant a lot to them in life.

☠ When 37-year-old oil heiress Sandra Ilene West died in 1977, she was buried in her blue 1964 Ferrari 330 America sports car. The entire car was encased in a box buried at the Alamo Masonic Cemetery in Texas, USA.

☠ Reuben John Smith was buried in 1899. He was seated in an oak and leather reclining chair, along with a warm coat and hat, and with a draughts board on his lap.

☠ Queen Victoria was buried with the bathrobe of her long-dead husband Prince Albert, as well as a plaster cast of his hand, and a lock of the hair of her servant John Brown.

☠ Horror-film actor Bela Lugosi was buried in 1956 wearing the black cape he had worn in a number of *Dracula* films.

ON THE MOVE

Some bodies have been dug up and moved over and over again. The record must surely belong to US President Abraham Lincoln, whose body has been moved a staggering 17 times.

NOT AGAIN!

☠ King Frederick the Great of Prussia asked to be buried at his palace of Sans Souci, but was buried instead in a church in Potsdam, Germany in 1786. In 1943, his body was moved first to Berlin and then to a salt mine to keep it safe during World War II. After the war, it was reburied in Hohenzollern Castle near Stuttgart. Finally, in 1991, he was reburied at his palace of Sans Souci.

☠ Eva Peron, the wife of the President of Argentina, died in 1952. Her body was preserved and was put on display in Argentina before it mysteriously disappeared. In 1971, it was revealed that it had been secretly taken to Italy and buried in Milan. The body was then moved to Spain, and in 1974, it returned to Argentina. That's a lot of air miles!

FIVE DEADLY PLACE NAMES

1. The Dead Sea, Israel And Jordan
Ten times saltier than the sea, this body of water deserves its name, as only a few bacteria are able to live there.

2. Death Valley, Arizona, USA
Death Valley is North America's driest and hottest spot. In 1849, travellers heading for California's gold fields suffered two months of 'hunger and thirst and an awful silence' there. As they left, one looked back and said, 'Goodbye, Death Valley.' The name stuck.

3. The Skeleton Coast, Namibia
This coast is littered with the bones of whales and the remains of shipwrecks. Vicious currents, fog, winds and rocks make it a deadly place for animals and humans.

4. Tombstone, Arizona, USA

This desert town sprung up because silver was discovered nearby. It soon got a reputation as one of the wildest places of the Wild West, and many cowboys and prospectors did end up in its cemeteries.

5. Murder Island, Nova Scotia, Canada

There are many different stories about the reasons for the name of this tiny island. Whichever is true, there is no doubt that in the last century, bleached human bones were often found on the stony beaches.

BRILLIANT LAST WORDS (MAYBE)

Albert Einstein, one of the most brilliant scientists who ever lived, mumbled a few words on his deathbed. They may have been amazing, but we'll never know. He spoke in his first language – German – and his American nurse didn't understand a word of it.

SKULL STORIES

☠ An adult human skull is made up of 22 different bones, but when babies are born, the bones are not fully grown and have soft areas between them, called fontanelles. As the baby's head grows, the bones join together, and the soft spots disappear, usually by the time a child is two years old.

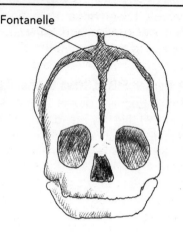

Fontanelle

CHEERS!

☠ In the 15th century, people on the island of Sumatra used human skulls as a form of money to buy goods with.

☠ Skulls found in Gough's Cave in Somerset, England, have been chiselled away to make drinking cups. The skull cups are thought to be almost 15,000 years old.

☠ Polish pianist André Tchaikovsky died in 1982 but got his dying wish fulfilled in 2008 when his skull was used by the actor David Tennant in a Royal Shakespeare Company performance of the play *Hamlet*.

☠ The Asmat people of New Guinea once believed in keeping their nearest and dearest close to them. Some sons used their dead fathers' skulls as pillows. Nowadays carved, wooden pillows are more usual.

I NEVER KNEW DAD HAD SUCH A HARD HEAD.

☠ In Bolivia, during the traditional festival of *Natitas*, people take skulls and decorate them with paints and flowers. They may use the skull of a loved one or take one from a grave that is no longer visited. The skulls are believed to offer protection against evil spirits and bad luck.

NO, YOU CAN'T DECORATE GRANNY'S SKULL. SHE'S NOT DEAD YET.

SERIOUSLY DANGEROUS SCIENCE

☠ Brilliant chemist Carl Scheele was the first to discover oxygen and also the first to identify the elements manganese, chlorine and tungsten. He tended to taste his new discoveries, which may have been unwise, as he is believed to have died of mercury and lead poisoning in 1786.

☠ Georg Wilhelm Richmann was an early student of electricity. Unfortunately, while examining an electrical experiment during a storm in 1753, he was struck by lightning that travelled through his apparatus and killed him instantly.

☠ Nobel-prize winning scientist, Marie Curie spent much of her life working with radioactive materials. She died from leukaemia, believed to have been caused by radiation exposure, in 1934.

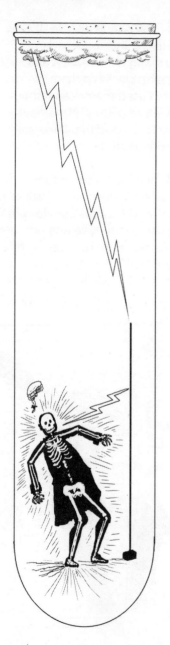

☠ Russian revolutionary and doctor Alexander Bogdanov was experimenting with blood transfusions when, in 1928, he gave himself a transfusion of blood from a student who had malaria and tuberculosis. He died shortly afterwards.

☠ Famous scientist and thinker Francis Bacon died in 1626 after a pioneering attempt to preserve food by freezing it. He spent too long outside packing snow into a chicken, contracted pneumonia, and died a week later.

I DON'T KNOW ABOUT SIR FRANCIS, BUT I THINK THE CHICKEN WILL LIVE.

DUMB, DUMB DEATHS

☠ Attila the Hun was the most feared warrior of his age, but one story tells that he died on his wedding night in 453 (he already had several wives), after drinking too much alcohol. He suffered a nosebleed and, too drunk to notice, choked to death on the blood.

☠ Martin of Aragon ruled not only Aragon, in Spain, but the islands of Sardinia, Corsica and Sicily, as well as being Count of Barcelona. In 1410, he is said to have died from a fatal laughing fit combined with very severe indigestion.

☠ Milo of Croton won wrestling competitions at five ancient Olympic Games and was renowned for his enormous strength … but not for his brains. Finding a tree trunk split with wedges, he put his hands into the gap to try to rip the trunk in two. Unfortunately, the wedges fell out, and Milo was trapped in the trunk. Unable to escape, he was devoured by a pack of wolves.

HAVING A BAD DAY?

☠ Clement Vallandigham was a US Congressman and a lawyer. While defending Thomas McGehan on a charge of murder, Vallandigham showed the court how the gunshot could have been accidental. He pulled out his own gun, thinking it was unloaded, and pulled the trigger. The gun fired and wounded Vallandigham, but the lawyer had proved his point. McGehan was set free. Vallandigham was not so lucky – he died of his injuries.

☠ Famous bourbon whisky-maker Jack Daniels kicked his metal safe in anger when he failed to open it. His toe became infected and the infection spread, killing him in 1911.

☠ In 207 BC, ancient Greek philosopher Chrysippus died. There are several stories about this. One says he got his donkey drunk and died of laughing as it tried to eat figs.

AND HE THINKS I'M DRUNK!

Jack The Ripper

Between 1888 and 1891, a terrifying series of murders shocked Victorian London. All the victims were women, and their bodies were cut open, possibly by someone with medical training.

There were many rumours going around about the unknown murderer. Some said he was a wealthy aristocrat from the highest level of British society – perhaps even a member of the royal family.

Over a hundred books have been written about the subject, and many experts have examined the evidence, but to this day, the identity of the real Jack the Ripper has never been revealed.

BED SPRING OR BULLET?

On 2nd July 1881, US President James Garfield was shot by a would-be assassin. He did not die at once, and all might have been well if the bullet could have been found and removed. Alexander Graham Bell, already a famous inventor, quickly made a metal detector and hurried to put it to use.

Unfortunately, the machine did not work properly. Some say the machine could not tell the difference between bullets, bed springs or the metal frame of the bed. Others claim that the President's doctor would not allow the inventor to do a thorough search.

The unfortunate Garfield lingered for 80 days, before dying of complications from an infection of the blood.

DANGER AT WORK

Some jobs turn out to be more gory, gruesome or downright dangerous than others.

Archbishop
A quiet, safe, indoor job? Not if you were an archbishop in Russia in the 16th century with Ivan the Terrible on the throne. It is said that in 1570, Archbishop Pimen of Novgorod was sewn into a bearskin and killed by a pack of hunting dogs.

Wife Of A Sultan
A life of luxury and glamour? Perhaps, but the 280 wives of Sultan Ibrahim I all suffered the same fate. They were each tied in a weighted sack and thrown into the River Bosphorus. It's a deep river, and not one of them survived.

Astronomer
Quiet work at night – a safe bet, surely? Not for Hsi and Ho, two ancient Chinese astronomers. They failed to predict a solar eclipse in the 22nd century BC and were beheaded on the orders of Emperor Chung K'ang.

Servant To A Queen

Protected by palace guards, surely a safe situation? Not if Egyptian Cleopatra was the queen in question. She researched poisons by testing them on prisoners who had been sentenced to death. When she decided to commit suicide by a poisonous snakebite, some of her servants were also ordered to kill themselves or face execution!

OH NO, YOUR MAJESTY, I COULDN'T GO BEFORE YOU!

The Top Job

So maybe the only safe job is the one at the top – ruler. Well, not necessarily. A Cambridge University professor in 2011 studied the lives and deaths of 1,513 European rulers between 600 and 1800 and discovered that almost a quarter of them died violently, mostly by being murdered.

BEWARE! DANGER OF DEATH

There are thousands of rules and regulations to help us keep safe from deadly accidents. Here are some warnings that maybe *should* have been given.

Beware Boomerang Chocs!

OH, MISS EDMUNDS, DIDN'T YOU LIKE THESE ONES EITHER?

Christiana Edmunds repeatedly bought chocolates from a shop in Brighton, England, laced them with strychnine poison, then returned them to the shop. Didn't anyone think this was odd? Many people became seriously ill, and a four-year-old boy died. Edmunds went on trial in 1872 and was sent to a lunatic asylum for the rest of her life.

YOU CAN'T WEAR THESE. THEY'RE A HEALTH HAZARD.

Always Wear Your Socks!

Calvin Coolidge Junior, the 15-year-old son of US President Calvin Coolidge, played tennis with his brother in June 1924. His tennis shoes, worn without socks, gave him a blister, which within days became infected. He died of blood poisoning eight days after the tennis match.

Be Careful Who You Marry!

In 17th-century Rome, fortune-teller Hieronyma Spara formed a secret organization to help women poison their wealthy husbands with arsenic and inherit their money. She was eventually caught and hanged.

Don't Dangle While Driving!

Isadora Duncan was a dancer who liked to be daring and dramatic. In 1927, she climbed into an open-topped car and, over-the-top as always, she waved goodbye with the words, 'Farewell, my friends! I go to glory!' Seconds later, she died when her long scarf became caught in the wheel and broke her neck.

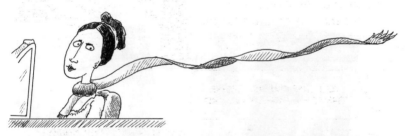

Poetry Can Be Perilous!

According to legend, ancient Chinese poet Li Bai (also known as Li Po) fell from his boat and drowned in the Yangtze River in 762 while trying to embrace and kiss the beautiful reflection of the moon in the water.

THE MURDEROUS DETAILS

Some murders become very famous – people can't wait to hear all the gory details. One such murder happened in Suffolk, England.

On 18th May 1827, a young woman called Maria Marten left home to meet her boyfriend, William Corder. She was never seen alive again.

Weeks and months went by, and Maria's father, sister and stepmother became worried. It was not like her to be away so long, especially as she had a little boy who was still at home. William Corder wrote to her family, saying that she was fine and that they were now married. The family became more and more suspicious. There was no word from Maria herself.

Almost a year after Maria disappeared, her stepmother claimed she had a dream that Maria had been killed and buried in the Red Barn nearby. She was so sure her dream was true, she persuaded her husband to go and search. Sure enough, Maria's body was found in a shallow grave.

William Corder was found and arrested in London. He went to trial and was sentenced to death. After he was hanged, with thousands of people watching, his body was cut open and put on display. Later, a book about the murder was produced and covered in leather made from Corder's skin. It can still be seen in a museum in Bury St Edmunds, Suffolk, where Corder was hanged.

As for the Red Barn, it was almost demolished by sightseers, who each took a piece home as a souvenir!

POISON PLOTS THROUGH THE AGES

Well, Well, Well

Some sneaky ancient Greeks who were attacking the town of Kirra in around 590 BC poisoned wells that supplied the town with water. They used a poisonous plant, the hellebore. The Kirrans became so ill that they were easy to defeat.

The ancient Assyrians used a fungus called ergot to poison enemy wells in the 6th century BC. The fungus could cause people to suffer hallucinations and die.

The Problem With Poison

Mithridates VI was the ruler of a kingdom in northern Turkey. He was so afraid of plots to poison him that he started taking an antidote every day to try to make himself immune.

When defeated by the Romans in 63 BC, he foolishly tried to commit suicide by taking poison. Needless to say, he failed. He had to force one of his own soldiers to kill him instead.

TOILET TROUBLE

According to legend, Edmund II, King of England, was murdered in 1016 when his attacker hid in the toilet below him and stabbed him with either a dagger or sharpened wooden pole. Ouch!

George II, a much later king of England, died from a blood vessel rupture while in the bathroom and either sitting on the toilet or falling off it – no one is certain – in 1760.

Roman Emperor Caracalla was stabbed to death with a sword in AD 217, after he had dismounted his horse to have a wee.

CREEPY CORPSE

Giovanni Aldini electrified onlookers in 1803 when he made the corpse of a dead murderer, George Forster, seemingly come back to life. Aldini had connected the body to a 120-volt battery, and Forster's fist clenched, his legs kicked about, and his jaw quivered. Very few people had seen electricity in action before.

Aldini's eerie experiment may have been in Mary Shelley's mind 12 years later when she began to write *Frankenstein*.

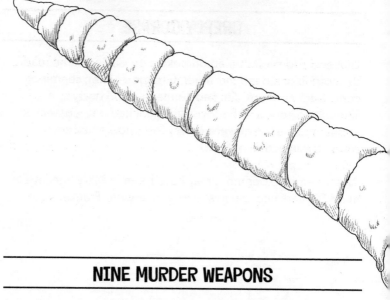

NINE MURDER WEAPONS

Believe it or not, all these have been used to commit murder:

☠ A pet turtle

☠ A poisoned umbrella tip

☠ A gun hidden in a lipstick

☠ A weed trimmer

☠ A thermometer

☠ A corkscrew

☠ A mobile phone fitted with a bomb

☠ A nail gun

☠ A chessboard.

SNATCHED BACK

Poet and painter Dante Gabriel Rossetti was devastated when his wife Elizabeth died in 1862. Before she was buried in Highgate Cemetery, London, England he tenderly placed in her coffin a handwritten copy of some poems he had been going to publish. Seven years later, Rossetti changed his mind, had her coffin exhumed and the poems taken out, and went on to publish them as a book in 1870.

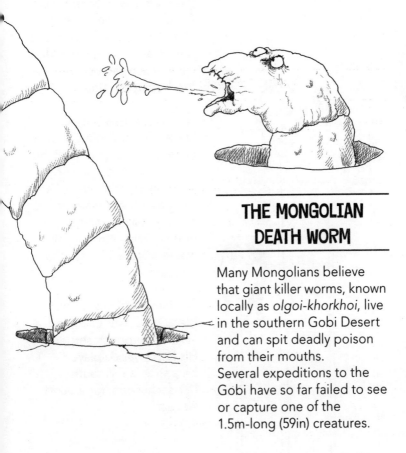

THE MONGOLIAN DEATH WORM

Many Mongolians believe that giant killer worms, known locally as *olgoi-khorkhoi*, live in the southern Gobi Desert and can spit deadly poison from their mouths.
Several expeditions to the Gobi have so far failed to see or capture one of the 1.5m-long (59in) creatures.

STICKY ENDS

Poking a pole or spear through a body part is called impaling. Over the years, many different people seem to have found the idea appealing.

☠ Around 3,000 years ago, parents of children who died in northern Scotland carried their remains to Sculptor's Cave near Lossiemouth. Many of the children's heads were placed on sticks in the cave, which can only be reached at low tide.

☠ 17th-century English leader Oliver Cromwell died of natural causes in 1658, but three years later, his body was dug up and hanged as a traitor. His head was cut off and placed on a spike outside Westminster Hall, where it stayed for around 20 years.

☠ Native American Chief Metacomet was executed in 1676 by European settlers. His head was displayed on a stick in Plymouth, Massachusetts, for around 20 years.

☠ Vlad III Dracul, Prince of Wallachia (1431–76) is sometimes called Vlad the Impaler. No wonder! He was known for killing people in nasty ways and particularly liked impaling their bodies on sticks to scare off enemies. His dark deeds may have been what inspired Bram Stoker to write the ultimate vampire story – *Dracula*.

MACABRE MUSEUM

The Musée Fragonard is a museum in Paris, France, that showcases some of the work of Honoré Fragonard. He made models using dead animals and people that had been skinned and posed in different positions. One of his most famous is *The Horseman of the Apocalypse* – a skinned dead man riding a skinned dead horse.

FATAL FIRSTS

1785: First Balloon Death

Jean-François Pilâtre de Rozier had two ballooning firsts. He was the first ever hot-air balloonist when he piloted the Montgolfier brothers' balloon in 1783. Two years later, he became the first balloonist to die as he tried to fly across the English Channel.

IS IT ME, OR IS IT GETTING SMALLER?

1830: First Railway Death

William Huskisson was a British Member of Parliament and a guest at the opening of the Manchester to Liverpool railway line. Unfortunately, he fell under the train's wheels and died nine hours later.

POOR CHAP DIDN'T STAND A CHANCE. IT MUST HAVE BEEN DOING AT LEAST 3 MPH.

1869: First Car Death

Irishwoman Mary Ward fell from a steam-powered car built by her cousins and broke her neck.

THEY OUGHT TO DO SOMETHING ABOUT THESE BUMPS!

1890: First Death By Electric Chair

William Kemmler, convicted of the axe murder of his girlfriend
Matilda Ziegler, became the first person to be executed by
electric chair at Auburn Prison in New York.

1904: First Death From Radiation

Clarence Madison Dally, an
assistant of the great inventor
Thomas Edison, experimented
with extremely powerful
X-rays. His hair and moustache
fell out and both his arms were
so damaged they had to be
amputated. He later died of
cancer caused by radiation.

NO! NOT THE
MOUSTACHE!

1908: First Aircraft Passenger Death

Orville Wright was the first man to fly in a powered plane in
1903. Five years later, he was performing a test flight with a
passenger, Lieutenant Thomas Selfridge, when the plane lost
control and nose-dived almost 25m (80ft) to the ground.
Wright survived, but his passenger did not.

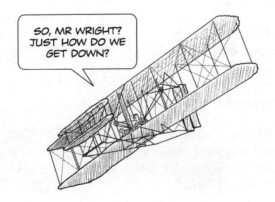

SO, MR WRIGHT?
JUST HOW DO WE
GET DOWN?

ASHES TO FLASHES

After cremation, your ashes can be buried … or they can be turned into something spectacular.

☠ Marvel Comics writer Mark Gruenwald's last request was for his ashes to be mixed with ink and the mixture used to print comic books. He got his wish and became part of a comic called *Squadron Supreme*.

☠ An American company takes just over 500g (1lb) of cremated ashes and makes 250 bullets with them. Loved ones can then fire them out of rifles, shotguns or other weapons.

☠ For those wanting to go up in a blaze of glory, a firework company will put some of a cremated person's ashes into four or more rockets for a sparkling display.

☠ An artist in the USA produces portraits of dead people and pets with some of their ashes mixed into the paints.

☠ Another company will heat cremated ashes or a lock of hair under pressure and create an artificial diamond.

☠ The ashes of Ed Headrick, who pioneered the Frisbee®, were mixed with plastic and used to make a limited edition memorial Frisbee®.

DIY MUMMIFICATION

When the ancient Egyptians made mummies (see page 14), they began by removing the body's insides, as they would be the first to decompose (rot). Scientists were astonished to find that some mummies in Japan still had their internal organs. The reason? These were Buddhist monks who had mummified themselves while they were still alive!

Here's how they did it:

1. For 1,000 days, the monk ate only seeds and nuts. He became very thin. The idea was to get rid of body fat, which was known to decompose quickly after death.

2. For the next 1,000 days, the monk ate only little bits of pine-tree bark and roots. Towards the end of this time, he started drinking a special tea made from the urushi tree. It was a poison that made the monk very ill, but it also meant that his whole body was poisonous, and insects wouldn't want to eat it after their death.

EWWW! DON'T EAT THAT ONE!

3. In the last stage, the monk, just skin and bones and very near death, was put in an underground tomb. He was given a bell and a straw to breathe through. Each day, the monk rang the bell. When the tomb was silent, his fellow monks knew he was dead and sealed up the breathing hole.

4. 1,000 days later, the other monks opened the tomb. Most of the time they found skeletons. Occasionally, they found a mummified body, which was then dressed in fine clothes and put in a shrine to be worshipped. They believed the monk had succeeded in becoming one with the Buddha and was very holy.

MILITARY MASSACRES

☠ In 1642, China was in the middle of a civil war. The city of Kaifeng on the bank of the Huang He River was under siege by rebels led by Li Zicheng. The governor of the city ordered that the dams holding back the waters of the river should be broken, hoping to break the siege. Instead, the massive flooding destroyed the city itself and is said to have killed as many as 300,000 people.

☠ Charlemagne, King of the Franks, was so angered at a rebellion by Anglo Saxons that in 782 he is said to have had 4,500 of his enemies beheaded in one day.

☠ During the Anglo-Afghan War (1839–42), a British Army force of 4,500 troops and 12,000 workers set out from Kabul to reach Jalalabad, 150km away. Waves of attacks from Afghan forces wiped them out, and only one man, a surgeon's assistant named William Brydon, survived.

☠ Asian warlord Timur lay siege to the city of Sivas, in Turkey, in 1401. He promised not to shed any blood if the city's defenders surrendered. When they did, he had over 3,000 of the city's soldiers buried alive. No actual blood was spilt, but they all died.

RUSSIAN REMAINS

Dying ... Dying ... Dead

A huge man with wild hair, a flowing beard, and the habit of eating with his fingers, Grigori Rasputin didn't look like the kind of person the Russian royal family would want to spend time with.

But Rasputin, sometimes called the 'Mad Monk', had many fans as a holy man with healing powers. Alexei, the only son of Tsar Nicolas II, was often ill, and Rasputin seemed to be able to help him.

Others did not like Rasputin's increasing influence, and Prince Yusopov decided he must die. This wasn't as easy as it sounds. Reports of his death are not all very reliable, but some say he was …

… given cakes full of poison

… shot four times

… beaten with clubs

… and finally, thrown into the icy River Neva.

When his body was found, it had water in the lungs, suggesting that Rasputin may have survived three murder attempts … only to drown.

Romanov Relations
Tsar Nicolas, his wife, four daughters and son did not fare much better. When the Bolsheviks overthrew the royal family, they were taken prisoner. In July 1918, they were killed. It was not until 2008 that scientists were able to prove that all the royal family died. Several distant relatives, including Prince Philip, husband of Queen Elizabeth II, gave DNA samples to help identify the remains.

SO YOU THINK YOU KNOW A ZOMBIE?

A zombie is a dead person who has been revived by magic, voodoo or witchcraft after burial. Fortunately, they only appear in horror movies and comics, and are sometimes known as the 'undead'. If you suspect one of your friends of being a zombie, here are ten tell-tale signs to look out for.

1. They stop eating salad and vegetables and start threatening to eat human brains.

2. Their skin becomes paler than usual.

3. They walk with a slow shuffle (okay, many teenagers do this, but even slower and more shuffly than usual).

4. They have 8th October ringed on their calendar or in their diary. This is World Zombie Day.

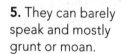

5. They can barely speak and mostly grunt or moan.

6. They have a bite mark on their skin that is infected. This is the possible cause of their zombie-dom.

7. They rarely brush their teeth or use deodorant, and they smell awful.

8. They are unable to do puzzles, crosswords or other tasks that require brain power.

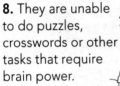

9. They don't sleep at all.

10. They move their arms and head in an uncoordinated way, and have trouble with fiddly things such as threading a needle.

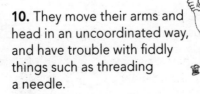

MAKE YOUR OWN BREAD OF THE DEAD

Pan de Muerto, or 'Bread of the Dead', is a sweet, doughy bread flavoured with orange, which is traditionally made on 1st November for the Mexican Day Of The Dead festival (see page 100). Here's how to make some Bread of the Dead rolls for you to enjoy all year round. This recipe makes seven tasty bread rolls.

You will need:

• 60ml (¼ cup) milk • 60g (½ stick) butter • 60ml (¼ cup) warm water plus a little extra for sprinkling • 400g (2 2/3 cups) white bread flour plus extra for kneading • 8g (1 sachet) baker's yeast • 75g caster sugar • 2 eggs (beaten) • zest of 1 orange (finely grated) • 2tsp anise seeds.

1. In a saucepan, heat the milk and butter until they are melted and combined. Then add the warm water and leave to cool down to a lukewarm temperature.

Warning: Ask an adult to help you when using the hob.

2. Mix 100g (⅔ cup) of the flour with all of the sugar and the yeast in a large mixing bowl. Add the butter, milk and water mixture, the eggs, orange zest and anise seed.

3. Stir, then add the remaining flour and use your hands to mix it all together until a soft dough forms.

4. Tip the dough on to a lightly floured surface. Use the heel of your hand to push into the dough, then stretch it back on itself before pushing into it again. Do this for about a minute.

5. Place the dough back in the mixing bowl, cover it with a clean towel and leave to rise for 90 minutes.

6. Tip the risen dough out on to a floured surface and use your fingertips to push the air out of it.

7. Split the dough into eight equal sized portions and shape seven of them into round rolls.

8. Break off little bits of the eighth piece of dough and roll them into thin sausage shapes and small balls between your hands. You need to get 14 thin sausages, and seven small balls of dough from this piece.

9. Sprinkle the rolls with a few drops of water, then lay two sausage shapes crossways over the top of each one, and top them with a small ball of dough. These are the bones for the bread of the dead.

10. Leave the rolls to rise again for an hour, then bake them in a preheated oven (180°C/350°F) for 20 minutes until golden.

Top Tip. Ask an adult to heat the juice of half an orange with 25g (⅛ cup) caster sugar until the sugar has dissolved. Brush this sweet and sticky glaze over your rolls for a truly tasty finish.

CANNIBALS!

Eating dead humans seems horrible to most of us, but some people take a different view.

Family Feast

The Wari tribe from the Amazon rainforest used to practise cannibalism on members of their own people. When a wife died, members of the husband's family would feast on her remains. When the Wari first had contact with European and modern South American customs, they were horrified by the idea of burying a dead loved one in the cold, dirty earth.

Eating The Enemy

French sailor Joseph Kabris lived with a cannibal tribe on the Pacific island of Nuku Hiva between 1796 and 1804. He reported that prisoners seized after battles were eaten. It seems the eyes, cheeks and brains were the favourite parts.

Dine Or Die

Some people have resorted to cannibalism in order to survive in extreme situations. Four sailors were marooned in a lifeboat in the Indian Ocean after their yacht, the *Mignonette*, sank in 1884. After 19 days at sea, two of the sailors killed the youngest, a cabin boy called Parker, and ate parts of him to survive. They were rescued some days later.

DEATH DEFEATED

Some people have made amazing recoveries when it seemed that death was the only outcome.

Firing Squad Fiasco

Wenseslao Moguel was sentenced to death by firing squad during the Mexican Revolution of 1915. He was shot a total of nine times by the gunmen but amazingly was still alive. He pretended to be dead until the firing squad left and managed to escape.

EXCUSE ME, I'M OVER HERE!

Defrosted

In 1985, a two-year-old boy, Michael Troche, was found frozen stiff in sub-zero temperatures in Milwaukee, USA. He had stopped breathing, ice crystals had formed under his skin, and a doctor pronounced him dead. Yet Michael eventually came round and made an amazing recovery.

A Narrow Escape

Magan Kanwat, a 72-year-old woman from Jaipur, India, was declared dead from a blood clot and was about to have her body burned on a funeral pyre when she was found to be breathing.

CAREFUL WITH THAT MATCH! SOMEONE COULD GET HURT.

Happy Landings

Juliane Koepcke was on board an aircraft struck by lightning in 1971. The lightning ripped the plane apart and killed all 92 passengers and crew, except 17-year-old Juliane, who fell, strapped in her seat, over 3,000m (1.8 miles) before crashing into the Amazon rainforest. In shock, with broken bones, no food and infections from insect bites, she walked for nine days through the jungle before being rescued and recovering fully.

YOU'RE LATE!

SINISTER SIEGE ENGINES

Catapults

Used by the ancient Greeks, Romans, Chinese and still in action in medieval times, a catapult's long arm flung heavy stones over long distances. The plague-ridden bodies of dead people or animals were also fired to spread disease.

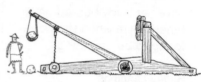

Trebuchet

These machines could hurl massive rocks weighing 100kg (220lbs) up and over castle walls, to crush buildings and people.

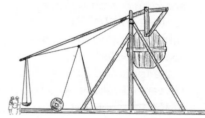

Ballista

This giant crossbow used tightly twisted animal hair to propel a weapon. Large wooden darts or giant arrows could sometimes skewer two people with one shot!

Battering Ram

Giant tree trunks, often with a heavy iron tip, were swung from chains to knock down a castle's walls. The soldiers or slaves swinging the trunk were in the direct firing line of arrows or, worse, giant vats of boiling oil, poured down on them by the enemy.

DEATH TO SPIES

Being a spy can be a dangerous career choice. When a spy gets caught out, things might well turn deadly.

Losing Her Head

Legendary female spy Mata Hari (real name Margaretha Zelle) was killed by firing squad. She was executed in 1917 by French forces, after being found guilty of spying for the Germans during World War I. Her body was not claimed by family members, and for a while her embalmed head was stored in the Museum of Anatomy in Paris.

Death Choice

During the American Revolutionary War, British spy John André was caught and sentenced to death. He pleaded with General George Washington, not for a pardon but to be killed by firing squad instead of hanging. His request was refused, and he was hanged in 1780.

SMERSH
In the 1940s, the Soviet Union had an organization that aimed to root out foreign spies and disloyal soldiers in its own armies, often torturing and sometimes killing them if found. The organization was known as SMERSH, from the Russian phrase *smert shpionam*, which means 'death to spies'.

Killing Coin
Some US spies in the 20th century were equipped with a 'dollar of death'. It looked like an ordinary American coin but it was hollow. Inside was either a tiny pill or a pin tipped with lethal poison. If he or she was captured, the spy often faced torture, as the captors tried to find out what the spy knew. The coin gave the spy the choice of suicide instead.

OW! WRONG
COIN!

DEAD ON DISPLAY

It is not only in the distant past that dead bodies have been put on display. Here are some that can be viewed today.

☠ A leader of the Russian Revolution in the 20th century, Vladimir Ilyich Lenin died in 1924. Russian embalmers preserved his body, which is on display in a special building in Moscow's Red Square. Each week, Lenin's skin is given a gentle scrub with bleach, and once every 18 months, he gets a full chemical bath while his clothes are washed and ironed.

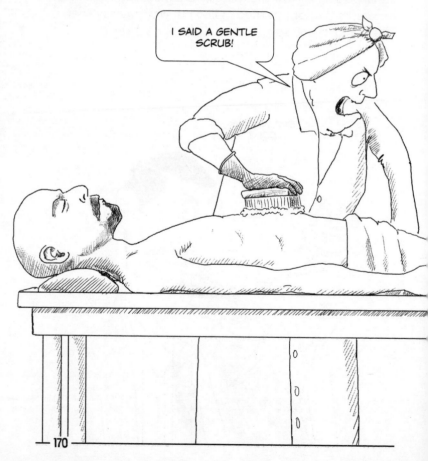

I SAID A GENTLE SCRUB!

☠ The body of Chinese leader Mao Zedong is often put on display in a glass case in his very own mausoleum in central Beijing, the capital city of China. When not on display, the body is kept fresh in a freezer under the mausoleum.

☠ Jeremy Bentham was a noted British thinker. His dead but preserved body (minus the head, which has been replaced by a wax one) is dressed in a suit and sits on a chair in a special cabinet at University College in London.
His mummified head is kept locked away in a special safe within the University.

MORE DUMB DEATHS

☠ During combat in the Arctic Ocean in 1942, the Royal Navy cruiser HMS *Trinidad* fired a faulty torpedo. The weapon headed off in a circle and returned to strike the ship, killing 32 people.

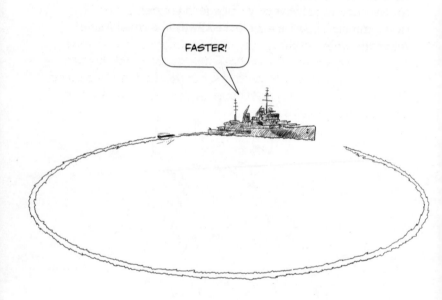

☠ Charles VIII, the King of France, was in a rush to watch a game of real tennis – a game played indoors – when he bashed his head on a stone doorway. He died only a few hours later.

☠ Allan Pinkerton, founder of the famous American Pinkerton Detective Agency, died in 1884 after biting his tongue. Untreated, the wound in his tongue became infected with gangrene, and he died a few weeks later.

☠ Yusuf Ismail was a famed Turkish wrestler who toured Europe and the USA. He died in 1898, when the ship he was travelling on, the SS *La Bourgogne*, sank. It is said that, after helping women and children leave the boat, Ismail drowned because he was weighed down by his large money belt. It was full of heavy coins – his wrestling prize money.

☠ Zishe (Siegmund) Breitbart, a famous circus strongman, survived having stones broken by sledgehammers on his chest during his act. He died in 1925 after another feat of strength, when he showed that he could drive an iron spike through five 2.5cm-thick (1in) oak boards using only his bare hands. That part was no problem, but he accidentally pierced his knee with the rusty spike, and he died eight weeks later of blood poisoning as a result.

FANTASTIC FINAL RESTING PLACES

Good Reef

A company in the USA builds artificial underwater reefs that contain the ashes of dead people. The 'reef balls', as they are called, are placed on the ocean bed, where coral and other sea life grows around them.

Green Death

Eco-friendly burials are now very popular. The body is placed in a coffin made of cardboard or some other material that will decay quickly and harmlessly in the soil. Woodland areas are often used for these burials, creating beautiful, natural places where plants and wildlife can thrive.

Deep Freeze

'Cryonic suspension' is the preserving of a person's brain or their whole body in ultra-low temperatures – around -196°C (-320°F). The hope is that at some point in the future, medical advances will mean that they can be revived and the cause of death treated. No one knows if this will work, but some wealthy people think it is worth the gamble, even though it is incredibly expensive.

Alone On The Moon

Only one person has ever been laid to rest on the Moon. He was Dr Eugene Shoemaker, one of the astronomers who discovered the Shoemaker-Levy 9 Comet. He died in 1997, and the following year some of his ashes travelled on the unmanned space-probe *Lunar Prospector*. The space-probe's mission ended in 1999, when it was deliberately crashed into a crater near the Moon's south pole. The place was renamed 'Crater Shoemaker' in his honour.

Mountaineering is a dangerous pastime, and many mountaineers find their final resting place in high and remote places. There are at least 120 dead bodies on the slopes of Mount Everest in its 'death zone' – the top part of the mountain, lying over 8,000m (26,000ft) above sea-level. The bodies are preserved by the icy temperatures and remain frozen where they fell many years ago.

DEADLY DOCTORS

In the past, some medical methods made going to the doctor distinctly dangerous.

You Need This Like A Hole In The Head!
In some ancient civilizations, a bad headache was sometimes treated by giving you an even worse one. 'Trepanning' is the medical practice of making a hole in a patient's skull.

Nowadays, doctors know that relieving pressure after a head injury may actually be a good idea, but long ago the operation was done with rough tools and no pain-numbing drugs. Many patients must have died. The amazing thing is that some did not. Skulls have been found in which the wounds had begun to heal.

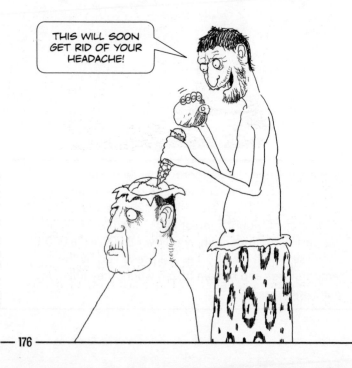

Blood Loss

For over 3,000 years, doctors thought that patients might be made better by losing blood! Bloodletting, as it was known, was done by cutting into a vein with a knife. There was a danger of the wound becoming infected, and after several sessions, some patients lost so much blood that they died anyway.

Asleep ... Forever

Until the 19ᵗʰ century, there was no general anaesthetic to make patients unconscious before an operation. Sleeping remedies were used, but most didn't work well and some were really deadly. A recipe from an Italian monastery in the year 800 included lettuce juice, mulberry juice, ivy, opium, henbane and hemlock. Those last three plants are deadly poisons!

TRAMPLED!

OI! WHERE ARE YOU GOING WITH MY CARPET?

After attacking the city of Baghdad, in modern day Iraq, in 1258, Mongol leader Hulagu Khan (grandson of warlord Ghengis Khan) captured the city's ruler. He had his captive tied up in a large rug. He was then carried out into a field and trampled to death by horses.

MAD, BAD AND MADAGASCAN

After the death of her husband Radama I in 1828, Queen Ranavalona I of Madagascar seized power. She began by executing all her potential rivals, including her dead husband's mother, daughter and nephew. She executed some islanders who practised Christianity, and introduced many tough new punishments for crimes. These included branding with hot irons and having to eat the highly poisonous nuts of the tangena shrub.

It was a relief to her subjects when she finally died in 1861.

BLOODSTAIN BUSINESS

A Scottish doctor named John Glaister (1892–1971) felt that more could be learned from bloodstains if they could be grouped and described. He suggested six different kinds of bloodstain, which could help investigators find out more about how deaths had occured.

☠ Drops on a horizontal surface, such as a floor or table.

☠ Splashes, from blood flying through the air and hitting a surface at an angle.

☠ Pools around the body.

☠ Smears left by a bleeding person moving.

☠ Spurts from a major blood vessel.

☠ Trails of blood from a body being carried or dragged.

FATAL FLOODS

Beer!

The London Beer Flood of 1814 sounds as if it might have been fun for adults, but when tanks at a brewery on Tottenham Court Road burst, over one million litres (over 200,000 gallons) of beer flooded the street, killing at least nine people.

Molasses!

The Great Boston Molasses Flood occurred in 1919. Massive waves of molasses (a thick, dark, sugary syrup) flowed at speeds of over 50km/h (over 30mph) after a giant storage tank broke. Around 21 people met a particularly sticky end.

BOILING BODIES

In 1531, King Henry VIII of England made boiling in water a punishment for people found guilty of poisoning. The Bishop of Rochester's cook, who poisoned two people, was boiled to death the following year. The last person to be executed in Britain by boiling was a maid called Margaret Davey in 1542.

In the 15th century, people who forged money in the Dutch town of Deventer were likely to be boiled alive in oil in a large copper kettle. The kettle is still on display in the town.

Not all guests who checked into the Ostrich Inn in the 17th century checked out alive. The owner of the hotel in Colnbrook, just west of London, England had a trapdoor installed in the inn's best guest room. The trapdoor would drop a guest straight into a cauldron of boiling water in the kitchens below, allowing the innkeeper to steal all his belongings.

MURDER
MYSTERY #4

The Dyatlov Pass Incident

In 1959, a search party looking for nine missing
ski-hikers on the Russian mountain Kholt Syakhl found
a grisly scene.

All nine hikers were dead, some battered with fractured
skulls and broken ribs, while others were just in their
underwear despite the intense cold.

There were large traces of radiation on some
of their clothes, and one of the dead bodies had its
tongue missing.

The official report said that their deaths were caused
by 'a compelling unknown force'. Aliens? Wild animals?
A secret atomic experiment? To this day, no one knows.

MISSING ... PRESUMED DEAD

Sometimes, people seem to vanish without a trace, and no dead body is ever found. Here are some of the most mysterious missing persons.

☠ Famous explorer Percy Fawcett and his expedition disappeared in 1925 while searching for a fabled ancient city in the rainforests of Brazil. More than a hundred people have died searching for Fawcett and his team.

WELL, WE'VE TRACED FAWCETT'S EXPEDITION TO HERE. NOW WHAT?

☠ Amelia Earhart, a famous female pilot, disappeared in 1937 over the Pacific Ocean, while flying her Lockheed Electra aircraft. No trace of the plane or Earhart have been recovered.

☠ Australian Prime Minister Harold Holt was a strong swimmer, yet he disappeared off Cheviot Beach, Australia, in 1967. His body was never found.

☠ Richard Bingham, 7th Earl of Lucan, known as Lord Lucan, disappeared in 1974, after his children's nanny was found dead at his home in London, England.

THE FACES OF DEATH

Death masks are made by moulding wax or plaster over the face of a dead person. They may be used to make statues or more copies of the mask.

Famous Faces

The death mask of Oliver Cromwell is on display at Warwick Castle, England, and that of Napoleon Bonaparte can be seen at the British Museum in London. Across the Atlantic Ocean, you can see the death mask of Native American Chief Sitting Bull at the West Point Museum in New York State, USA.

Oliver Cromwell

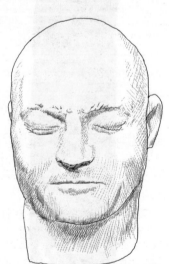

Ned Kelly

Other famous people who have had death masks made include suspense film-maker Alfred Hitchcock, US President Abraham Lincoln, composer Ludwig von Beethoven, and two infamous criminals – the Australian Ned Kelly and a US bank robber named John Dillinger.

Before The Museum ...

We now think of Madame Tussaud as a chain of waxwork museums, but Madame Tussaud was a real person. Born in 1761, she became involved in the French Revolution and was sentenced to death. She was set free on the condition that she made wax death masks of executed people, including King Louis XVI, and his wife, Queen Marie-Antoinette. She had the horrible job of searching through piles of dead body parts to find the right heads.

WHY IS THE ONE YOU WANT ALWAYS AT THE BOTTOM?

A FLY'S FUNERAL

Ancient Roman poet Vergil (also known as Virgil or Publius Vergilius Maro) gave a lavish funeral for a fly he claimed was his pet. He paid for a full orchestra to play at the fly's burial in the gardens surrounding Vergil's villa. Was Vergil nuts? No, he was very, very clever. Under Roman laws, lands that were burial grounds did not have to pay large taxes to the government.

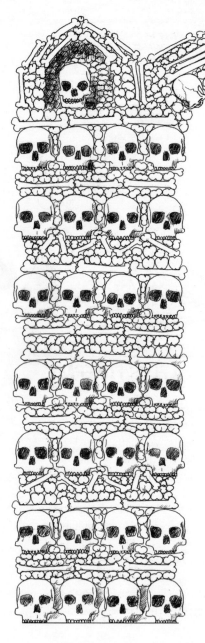

INFAMOUS OSSUARIES

An 'ossuary' is a place where bones are kept. Here are five extraordinary ones.

1. The Capela dos Ossos is a chapel in Evora, Portugal. It's decorated inside with the skulls and bones of about 5,000 dead people, mostly monks.

2. The Skull Chapel in Czermna, Poland, contains the skulls of some 3,000 dead people in its walls, with hundreds of shin bones making up the ceiling. And that's not all. In the cellar below the small chapel can be found a further 21,000 human skulls.

3. In the Spanish village of Wamba, the Church of Santa Maria contains organized piles of around 1,000 skulls of local people who died between the 12th and 18th centuries.

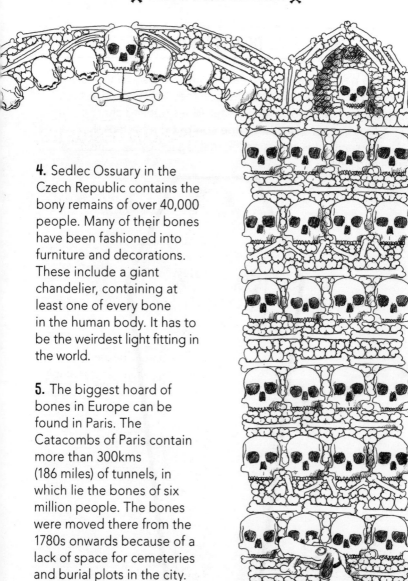

4. Sedlec Ossuary in the Czech Republic contains the bony remains of over 40,000 people. Many of their bones have been fashioned into furniture and decorations. These include a giant chandelier, containing at least one of every bone in the human body. It has to be the weirdest light fitting in the world.

5. The biggest hoard of bones in Europe can be found in Paris. The Catacombs of Paris contain more than 300kms (186 miles) of tunnels, in which lie the bones of six million people. The bones were moved there from the 1780s onwards because of a lack of space for cemeteries and burial plots in the city.

DEATH MYTH

Some people say that a person's fingernails and toenails keep growing after death. In fact, they don't. What actually happens is the body dehydrates (dries up) and shrinks a little, so that the nails stay the same size but the flesh of the fingers and toes gets smaller, making it look as if the nails have grown.

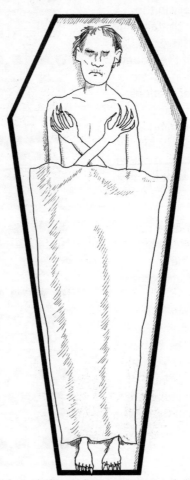

MURDER MYSTERY #5

Ghost Ship

The *Mary Celeste*, an American sailing ship, was found floating in the Atlantic Ocean between Portugal and the Azores islands in 1872. Its cargo of 1,700 barrels of alcohol was all present, as were the crew's valuables, clothes and other possessions. But the entire crew, passengers, and the ship's experienced captain, Benjamin Spooner Briggs, were all missing. The crew hadn't jumped ship because of a lack of food or water, as there were supplies for six months aboard. And with the cargo and valuables intact, piracy seems out of the question.

So what did happen? Were the crew and passengers taken away and murdered? To this day, no one is certain.

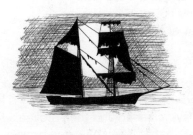

FASCINATING FUNERALS

Some cultures deal with their dead in interesting and unusual ways. Read on to find out more.

☠ The Toraja people, who live on the Indonesian island of Sulawesi, kill water buffalo when a person dies. The more important the person, the longer the funeral lasts and the more animals are sacrificed.

☠ In the past, the Toraja used to bury babies who died inside the trunks of living trees, believing that the child might continue to grow with the tree.

☠ The Bo people of south-west China used coffins to hold a dead body but then hung the coffin over the edge of a steep cliff. The coffins stayed there as long as the ropes used to lower them lasted.

☠ In Tibet, *jhator* – 'sky burial' – is still practised by some followers of Buddhism. A dead person's body is left out in the open for a few days, cleaned and then broken and cut into a number of pieces so that it can be eaten by wild creatures.

☠ Zoroastrians are followers of a religion that began in ancient Iran around 3,500 years ago. They believe that when a body dies, it is unclean, so it is placed on a structure called a *dokhma*, or 'tower of silence', in the open air. There the body is exposed to the sun and eaten by birds of prey.

☠ In the past, when some Hindu men died, their wives would perform *suttee* (or *sati*). When the husband's body was burned on a funeral pyre, the wife would join him and would be burned alive. *Suttee* was never widely practised and was made illegal in 1829, but a few cases have happened since.

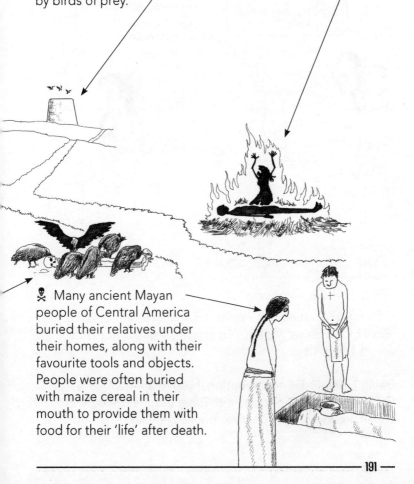

☠ Many ancient Mayan people of Central America buried their relatives under their homes, along with their favourite tools and objects. People were often buried with maize cereal in their mouth to provide them with food for their 'life' after death.

BURNING ISSUES

Cremation is a very common way of dealing with dead bodies. A corpse is placed in a special furnace that is heated to incredibly high temperatures. The hottest ones reach temperatures of up to 1,093°C (2,000°F) – hot enough to melt copper.

A typical cremation reduces an adult man to about 2.7kg (6lbs) of 'cremains' – cremated remains – and a woman to about 1.8kg (4lbs).

Being cremated is not an option if you're a Muslim or an Orthodox Jew. It's popular with other people, though. In Japan around 99% of people choose cremation.

THE BODY FARM

The original body farm was set up as a department of the University of Tennessee in the 1980s. Surrounded by high wire fences, lots of bodies are left in different conditions and are studied to see how they decompose – providing useful information for people who investigate deaths, such as police officers and forensic pathologists (who examine dead bodies to try and find out how they died). People who want their bodies to be useful in this way after death fill in forms to give their permission.

SO WHAT ARE YOU PLANTING THIS YEAR, FARMER JONES?

SACRIFICE!

In the past, people of all ages have been killed as sacrifices to gods or spirits. Sacrifices occurred for lots of reasons, for example, to ask the gods for a good harvest or a victory in a forthcoming battle. If you need to give a god a valuable present, what could be more precious than a human life?

COME BACK! IT'S A GREAT HONOUR!

☠ The Pawnee Native American people sometimes sacrificed a young girl during their Morning Star ceremony in spring. She would be shot through the heart with a special arrow and clubbed around the head during the ceremony.

☠ In the 17th and 18th centuries, the Kingdom of Dahomey in western Africa held ceremonies each year to remember its former kings. During the lengthy celebrations, slaves and enemies captured in battle were sacrificed.

☠ The Aztecs in Central America feared their god Tlaloc, who they believed caused rains, floods, drought and lightning. They sacrificed young children to keep Tlaloc happy. The Aztecs also sacrificed people to make sure that the Sun rose every morning and to celebrate the building of a new temple. An Aztec priest would sometimes rip the still-beating heart of a victim out and hold it up to the sky.

CUT OFF YOUR NOSE ...

During the 16th century, Japan invaded Korea, sparking a brutal war. Japanese warlords used to bring back severed heads or face parts of enemies as proof of their success. In 1983, a tomb was discovered in Japan, which contained around 20,000 noses of Koreans killed in the invasion. The noses were handed back to Korea in 1992, where they were cremated.

DEADLY DEITIES

Here is a collection of gods and other supernatural figures connected with death from different religions and cultures all over the world.

Cerberus, Ancient Greece And Rome
A three-headed dog who guards the gates to the Underworld (Hades), where the souls of dead people go.

Hine-nui-te-po, New Zealand And Polynesia
The goddess of death, night and darkness, queen of the underworld.

Santa Muerte, Mexico
A human skeleton, often carrying a globe and a staff with a curved blade called a scythe.

Asto Vidatu, Persia
A demon of death who chases souls with a noose.

Banshee, Ireland
A female fairy or spirit who appears and wails when someone in a family is soon to die.

Anubis, Ancient Egypt

A two-legged figure with the head of a jackal who is the god of mummifying dead people and accompanying their souls on their journey into the afterlife.

Yama, India

The Hindu lord of death, often shown as green, with red eyes, and riding a black buffalo. He weighs up the good and bad deeds a dead person has done throughout their life.

The Grim Reaper, Europe

A cloaked figure who carries a scythe and an hourglass to show you that your time is running out.

DEATHS IN THE WILD WEST

It was known as the land of cowboys, outlaws and gunslingers, so it's no surprise that the Wild West in the USA was a hotspot for death!

☠ John Wesley Hardin was a notorious Wild West gunfighter who killed between 27 and 42 men before being sent to prison. Hardin was eventually shot and killed in 1895 by another gunman, John Selman, while playing dice in the Acme Saloon in El Paso, Texas.

☠ While playing poker in a saloon in Deadwood, South Dakota, famous gunslinger James 'Wild Bill' Hickok was shot dead from behind by Jack McCall. As he fell, the playing cards he was holding were the ace of clubs, the ace of spades and a pair of eights. This is known to this day as the 'Dead Man's Hand'.

☠ In 1891, an infamous gunfight broke out near the OK Corral in the mining town of Tombstone, Arizona. It lasted less than a minute, but the brothers Wyatt, Virgil and Morgan Earp and their pal, gunslinger Doc Holliday, killed three men. The men were buried at Boot Hill Cemetery – so named because many of those buried there died sudden, violent deaths … with their boots on.

☠ Not all famous gunfighters died at the hands of others. William Sidney Light, a former deputy sheriff turned criminal, accidentally shot himself when riding on a train in 1893. He pulled the trigger of the gun in his pocket by mistake, shooting a large hole in his leg. He died of massive blood loss shortly after.

☠ George Parrot, also known as Big Nose George, was an outlaw from Wyoming. He was arrested and executed for the murder of two law enforcers, but his story doesn't end there. The doctor examining his corpse after execution had George's skin stripped from his body and made into shoes, which he wore for several years afterwards. Now that's some frightful footwear!

GHASTLY GHOSTS

No one has ever proved that ghosts exist, but many people believe that the spirits of dead people can appear in ghostly form to the living.

DON'T WORRY, I'LL TAKE THE NEXT ONE.

Haunting Hotspots
Most ghosts are sighted in places where a murder or a tragic accident has occurred. The 13 people who died in a lift during a fire at the Joelma Building in Sao Paolo, Brazil, in 1974, are said to haunt the building to this day.

A Really Spooky Ship
One of the most haunted locations in the United States is not a house or a hotel but a ship – the retired cruise liner *Queen Mary*. A number of different ghosts have been sighted on the ship. These include a girl who drowned in one of the ship's swimming pools and a young seaman who was crushed and died in engine room 13.

Perhaps It's A Poltergeist
The first recorded 'poltergeist' – an invisible ghost or force that moves objects and makes noises – was documented in 856 in Germany. It is said to have banged walls, lit fires and thrown stones.

WHO DID THAT?

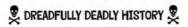

A Regular Visitor
The ghost of one of Henry VIII's wives, Anne Boleyn, is believed to hold the record for the most sightings – some 30,000 since her execution in 1536.

TEN TELL-TALE SIGNS OF A HAUNTED HOUSE

Some people believe that dead people can visit the living, and they reckon that there are signs to look out for. (Others, of course, think there are perfectly good non-ghostly explanations for all of them.)

1. Radios and TVs turning on and off or lights flickering.

2. Feelings of being touched by something invisible.

3. Water taps turning on and off by themselves.

4. Sudden cold spots in a room. (It is said that ghosts take energy from their surroundings.)

5. Unexplained smells appearing in a room, such as a perfume no one in the house uses.

6. Pets acting strangely, such as cats hissing at seemingly empty spaces or dogs refusing to enter a room.

7. Sudden shadows moving around the room.

8. Cupboard doors opening and closing by themselves.

9. Muffled voices, screams or other unexplained sounds.

10. Objects rising from tables by themselves.

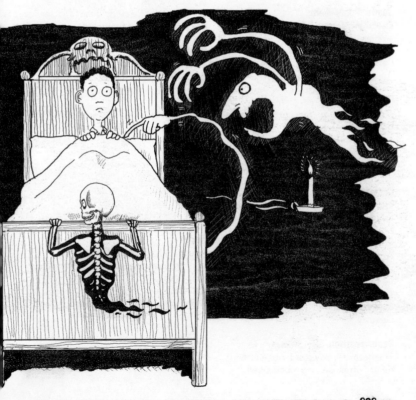

DREADFULLY DEADLY DEFINITIONS

Amputate
Having an injured or infected body part cut off.

Assassin
Someone who kills an important person in a surprise attack.

Bequeath
To pass on something via a will.

Buboes
Painful swollen lumps around the armpits and groin. A symptom of the Bubonic Plague.

Capital Punishment
Executing someone convicted of a crime.

Catacomb
An underground cemetery.

Cemetery
A place where bodies are taken to be buried.

Corpse
A dead body.

Cremation
The process of burning a dead body to ashes.

DNA
A set of instructions found in all living things, which tells them how to function.

Deceased
Dead.

Decomposition
The breaking down of a body after death, often causing a bad smell.

Epidemic
A widespread illness or infection.

Execution
Legally killing someone as a way of punishing them.

Exhumation
Digging up a buried body.

Forensic Pathologist
Someone who examines dead bodies to find out how they died.

Funeral Pyre
A pile of wood or other material that burns on which a body is laid and set fire to as part of a funeral rite.

Gangrene
What happens when tissue in the body dies due to lack of bloodflow.

Mace
A large club with spikes on the end of it, used as a weapon.

Mourning
Grieving for someone who has recently died.

Murder
Deliberately killing someone else.

Noose
A loop of rope placed around the neck of someone who will be hanged.

Sacrifice
A person or animal who gives up their life for something else.

Suicide
Deliberately killing yourself.

INDEX